Roaring Roadsters #2

By Don Radbruch

Cover Art By Bob McCoy

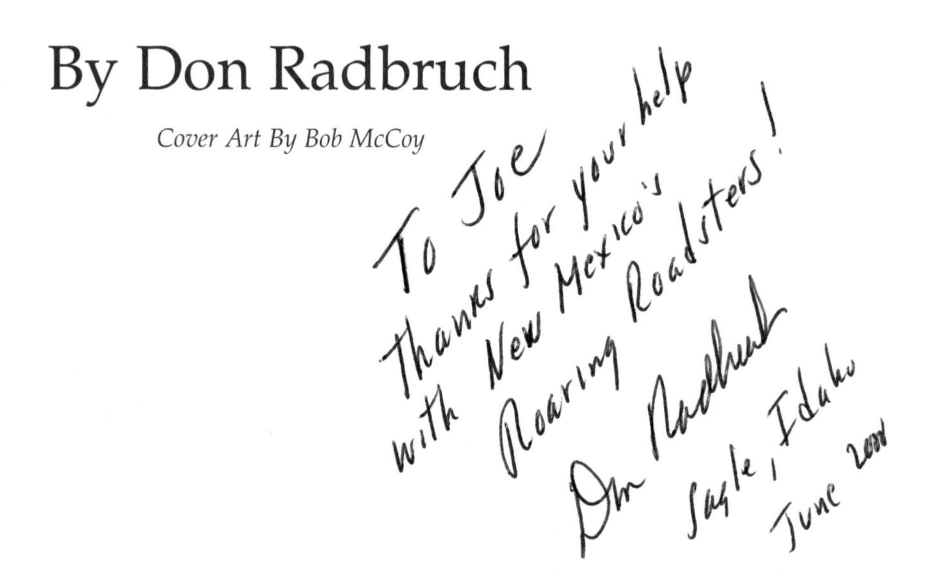

PRINTED AND BOUND IN THE UNITED STATES OF AMERICA

First produced in 2000 by Hot Rod Library, Inc., 991 N. Main St., Driggs, ID 83422.

ISBN 1-878772-00-7

Printed and bound in the United States of America

Author	DON RADBRUCH
Publisher	LEROI TEX SMITH
Editor	JIM CLARK
Technical Editor	RON CERIDONO
Art Director	BOB REECE

Roaring Roadsters #2

TABLE OF CONTENTS

About Roaring Roadsters II

In a way research for *Roaring Roadsters II* was easier than for the first book. People who helped with *Roaring Roadsters* continued to help by providing leads that turned up other roadster people. Also, readers of *Roaring Roadsters* contacted me and offered to help with the new book.

A successful approach that worked last time was continued. "Letters to the Editor", asking for information, were written to newspapers all over the country. These letters were especially helpful in turning up information on roadster racing that was missing from the first book. Columnists in publications like *National Speed Sport News* and *The Alternate* were kind enough to write pleas for hard-to-find information that helped a lot.

I wrote about 1500 personal letters during the research period, most were answered. There were lots of phone calls and contacts were made at vintage races in Oregon, Idaho, California and Kansas. Scores of people were kind enough to lend me nearly 2000 roadster photos.

As with *Roaring Roadsters* this book would not have happened without the help of a lot of wonderful racing people all over the country. I'd have to guess that close to 400 people contributed at least something to *Roaring Roadsters II*. Thank you, one and all.

The following people provided exceptional help hopefully I haven t missed anybody.

Gail Alloway
Andy Anderson
Don Anderson
Emil Andres
Neal Arndt
Mike Ashley
Art Bagnel
Bob Barkhimer
Bob Bartlett
Wade Bedell
Mike Bell
Peter Bennett
Dave Boon
Buck Bowers
Ken Boydstun
Ray Boyles
Allan Brown
Dave Burt
Leroy Byers
Per-Olof Carlsson
Emmet Carpenter
Joe Cawley
Jim Chini
Paul Clapper
Dave Cole
Vince and Mary Conrad
Bruce Craig
Lee Davis
Mike De Lany
Phyllis and Joe Devine
Marian Dinwiddie
Tom Donahue
Dick Downs
Mark Downing
Al Drake
Ray Eaton
Chris Economaki
Lou Ensworth
Rod Eschenburg
Dale Fairfax
Bob Fanning
Pike Green
Howard Gardner
Bob Garner
Jim Gessford
Don Gilchrest
Golden Wheels Members
Jack Greiner
Jon Gullihier
Bob Hart
Buddy Herdon
Ray Hiatt
Eileen Higginson
Bill Hill
Warren Hokinson
Leu Holland
Dan Iandola
John Jackson
Walt James
Brandon Johnston
Paul Kamm
Johnny Klann
Jay Koch
John Kozub
Perry Kratchmer
Loren Kreck
Galen Kurth
Chick Lastiri
Billy Lee
Punch Lemburg
Lloyd Libert
Dick Liebfritz
Marty Little
Johnny Lomonto
Lompoc Historical Society
Ted Mahoney
Jack Martin
Dick Mc Clung
Mick Michaels
Phyllis Morton
Tommy Morrow
Tom Motter
Herman Mox
John Mulleneix
Derald Nye
Don O'Riley (Urgo)
Clyde Palmer
Lynn Paxton
Jim Penney
Tom Poore
Harvey Porter
Dick Postier
Brian Pratt
Diane Radbruch
Don Radbruch
Nancy Radbruch
Dickie Reese
Stan Reynolds
Dick Richardson
Kevin Richardson
Eric Rickman
Rocky Rockwell
Jack Rook
Jim Ruth
Rosie Roussel
Troy Ruttman
Mary Ryan
Doris Schindler
Henry Schroeder
Dick Schultz
Greg Sharp
Jeff Sharpe
Bob Sheldon
Sonny Shillito
George Shippers
Bob Silvia
Gordy Shuck
Rich Slawson
Les Smiley
Bill Smith
Tex Smith
Ken Stansberry
Gordy Sutherland
Al Swenson
Carl Sweigart
Alice Van Hosen
Ray Valasck
Bob Veith
Bill Warden
John Way
Monte Wellendorf
Paul Weisner
Gordon White
Howard White
R.C. Whitwell
Nelson Weirenga
Andy Wilson
Herchel Wagner
Buyrl Ward
Tom Ward
Bernie Wehrner
Crocky Wright
Harry Yost

A special "thank you" to my wife, Naida, for doing the spelling corrections, proofreading, fixing awkward sentences and for adding 99% of the commas.

About The Author

I've been a racing fan forever. It all started in the 1930s in the San Francisco Bay Area where my folks, and my uncle, took me to big car, midget and roadster races. I saw the great drivers of the era race. Men like Rex Mays, Al Gordon, Duane Carter and Fred Agabashian were my heroes. I now know that this hooked me on racing for life.

World War II interrupted whatever thoughts I had about driving and I wound up in the Infantry in Germany. After the war there was college. I remained a racing fan and also took photos at the races. Becoming a driver just sort of happened in 1948 when I had a rather junky, street hot rod. My brother Les and I converted it to a track car—dumb move! For the money we spent we could have purchased a competitive car. Instead we wound up with an overpriced, overweight and uncompetitive car. On top of this I had no natural talent for driving. I must have been stubborn (I think my wife will confirm this today) so I stuck with it, and even with good ole #74, until I learned to drive a racecar.

Better roadsters followed and during the next couple of years I was at least competitive. When roadster racing started to die out in 1950 I switched to the sprints and that winter Les and I built our own Mercury powered sprinter. We even had some advanced ideas and used a primitive form of the space-frame in use today. This car won us an American Racing Association (now Northern Auto Racing Club) championship. There were thoughts of heading east for AAA racing, but not enough money to come up with an Offy—in retrospect I know I wasn't brave enough anyway.

Racing continued to be a big part of my life until 1967. I quit the sprints in 1953 and pretty well stuck to the Bay Cities Racing Association indoor midgets. There was also some sports car racing—for this I had financial backing from my boss and, for a time, enjoyed having the best car. This sure makes it a lot easier to win!

The author today in the Tritten Special.

I have always been interested in racing history and even wrote historical articles for *Speed Age* ages ago. In the past five or so years I've become as hooked on racing history as I was on racecars. The first track roadster book, *Roaring Roadsters,* was finished about three years ago and, almost immediately, work was started on this book. I also do writing for Phyllis Devine's, *The Alternate*, and Charlie Yapp's, *Secrets* as well as other publications and vintage club newsletters. It keeps me more than busy and, with *Roaring Roadsters II* out of the way, I'll devote more time to this sort of thing, plus start some new research projects. Racing hooked me 65 years ago and I'm glad.

Currently I'm retired with all the money I made racing—yeah, sure!!! My wife Naida and I have a house in the forest south of Sandpoint (Sagle) in Northern Idaho. We share this with our five cats Maxwell, Sophie, Harley, Bridget and Leo plus dog, Gregory.

—Don Radbruch

Dedication

If you live long enough, everything you've ever loved will be sullied.

—Ernest Hemingway

In today's world we constantly watch our sports heroes sullied. Fortunately our racing heroes have, for the most part, escaped this stigma. Oh sure, there is insider information that some race drivers are not the nicest people, but we can be thankful that they behave far better than stars of other sports.

My racing hero is, and always will be, Rex Mays. He was the first driver who started in the roadsters to make it to Indy. Even though he never won The 500, he dominated racing in the 1930s and 1940s. He was a two time national champion. Off the track he didn't drink, smoke or even cuss. Rex Mays was easy for me to idolize when I was a kid and this admiration was carried on when I grew up. To this day I can remember exactly where I was and what I was doing at the moment I heard of his death in 1949.

The best documentation of Rex Mays' career comes from a University of Southern California Masters Thesis (and soon to be published book) by Robert M. Schilling, *Pole Position: A Biography of American Race Driver Rex Mays.* Schilling traces Mays' racing exploits and personal life from the roadsters until his tragic death at Del Mar, California on November 6, 1949. The following is quoted from the Shilling manuscript:

"Rex Mays III (usually thought of as Rex Jr.) is amazed that, after 40 years, people will come up to him and speak of knowing his father, of seeing him race. All of them make some variation of the comment 'Your father was the most wonderful man in the world.' Even after all these years nothing negative about Rex Mays has ever come up. Rex Mays remains a hero."

Hemingway wrote that, 'If you live long enough, everything you've ever loved will be sullied'. Hemingway never met Rex Mays.

I humbly dedicate *Roaring Roadsters II* to my hero—Rex Mays.

Rex Mays. Del Mar, California, November 6, 1949. (Winkler Collection)

Rex Mays. Riverside, California. January 10, 1932. (Bob Chantland Collection)

What Is A **Track Roadster**

Somebody once said that the more you know about a subject the more you know what you don't know. This was probably Shakespeare or Hemingway and I'll bet he was talking about roadster racing. I'm supposed to be an authority on track roadster racing—here I am starting my second book on the subject and I find that I don't really know the definition of a track roadster. What is worse is that when all this began five years ago "knowing" what a track roadster was wasn't a problem. It was an open-wheeled car with a roadster body and a hopped-up engine. Now, five years later, I must admit it is not that easy—this is progress?

The problem with a simple definition of a track roadster comes from several different directions. In the 1930s Model T Ford races were held at hundreds of racetracks all over the country. Most of the Model Ts were roadsters and they were stripped of fenders and other body parts. They were probably supposed to have stock T engines and, hence, would not be track roadsters, but what if somebody cheated? Knowing racers, it is for sure there were a few cheaters so, by "definition", these become track roadsters.

Then there were the early "jalopies". Many of the races were on off-road courses, there were some coupes and sedans, but most of the cars were stripped roadsters. Can this be called a form of roadster racing?

In some areas of the country the "jalopies" ran on oval tracks, were strictly roadsters and had modified engines. The rules governing these cars were often very liberal and the roadster bodies were stripped to almost nothing—sometimes to really nothing. At what point does a roadster cease being a roadster?

So we have Model Ts that mostly weren't track roadsters. We have jalopies that did not run on an oval track and/or were sometimes stripped of any resemblance to a track roadster. Where do we go from here?

It seems best to revert to the dictionary meaning of a roadster and take it from there. The dictionary says that a roadster is "a single seated open conveyance." Applying a bit of logic, if this vehicle runs on a racetrack, it is therefore a track roadster. Or at least I'm going to say it is!

Some cars are very much on the fringe of "real" track roadster racing, but I've included them in *Roaring Roadsters II.* I've made no attempt to completely cover these "fringe" cars. A book or more could be written about them—especially the Model T races.

Alabama

Only a fraction of Alabama roadster racing has been unearthed. No doubt the following tale is typical of dozens of Alabama tracks that raced some form of roadsters.

This comes from a November 9, 1939 issue of *National Auto Racing News.* (This publication is now *National Speed Sport News.*) The headline of the article is "Unusual Meet at Summinton, Ala" and the byline is "Goldsmith". Mr. Goldsmith, obviously a regular contributor to the newspaper, relates how he came upon the races while motoring through Alabama on October 29, 1939. He stopped for gas at the tiny village of Summinton and was informed that there were auto races that afternoon at Summinton Speedway.

Summinton Speedway turned out to be located in a cow pasture complete with cows and haystacks. A rough oval was laid out around the cows and their hay, with a barbed wire fence to keep the bovines off of the track.

Goldsmith writes: "While I was sitting figuring out why a race track should be built there, a great clattering of tin reached my ears and, turning around I saw an old cutdown Model A Ford being towed out onto the track. Reaching for my box Brownie I was frozen in the act by the sudden zoom of a motor. Yes, it was coming from that jalopy, but I must admit that I first scanned the skies before being convinced."

This photo from microfilms of* National Auto Racing News *shows a field of cars lined up at Summinton in 1939. The cars appear comparable to prewar track roadsters in other parts of the country. (Johnny Wright Collection)

In due time eighteen "contraptions" arrived at the track, along with 2500 spectators. Goldsmith relates that most were cutdown V8s, but several had familiar DO and rockerarm heads (on Model A or B engines). Sam Sosmer was the star driver of the show and turned a short half-mile in the very respectable time of 27.4 seconds. Sosmer won the main as Shorty Goodwin flipped and suffered a broken leg.

Locals reported that the races had been going on every Sunday for a year and that in the near future they planned to build a grandstand.

Birmingham has now mostly swallowed up Summinton. A plea for further information sent to the racing columnist of the Birmingham newspaper was not answered. How many "Summintons" were there in Alabama?

Thanks to Brian Pratt of Burnaby, British Columbia for coming up with this information.

Alberta

The only roadster racing in the Canadian province of Alberta was Model T racing. The Alberta T racing was well organized and developed some good drivers and fast cars. Strangely enough the best years of this racing were during World War II.

Canada had already been at war for two years when, in 1941, the Lions Club in Calgary was seeking a means of raising money for wartime charities. Somebody came up with the idea of a Model T race. The Lions knew nothing about racing but the half-mile Victoria Park horse track was available in Calgary and 100 miles must have sounded like a nice round number so that was set as the distance. Modification of the Ts was allowed so most cars were stripped to near nothing and lowered for better handing.

A very lucky Stan Reynolds is surrounded by smiling faces at Calgary. The wheel hub broke just as Reynolds crossed the finish line for a big win.

Race day saw 12,000 fans in the grandstand and 33 cars in the starting field. It was a wild and woolly show as the Model Ts knocked down fences and ran into each other in the heavy dust. In mid-race a downpour hit and the dust became mud. After 15 recorded crashes and nearly four hours of racing Norman Price, in a 1924 T, was flagged the winner and awarded $250 first place money. The Lions raised $5000 for charity.

In 1942 the Lions were a wiser group and changed the format to three 15-mile heats and a ten-mile runoff for the winners. This time the races attracted 17,000 spectators, Don Robinson won the final heat and $100. A month later the Edmonton Lions Club

Stan Reynolds is shown leading the Canadian Model T Championship race at Calgary in 1947.

held a race and attracted a crowd of 8,000.

During the next several years annual events were held at Calgary, Edmonton and at Red Deer. For some drivers the T races were a one-time experience with near stock Model Ts. Other drivers competed in many races and their modified machines were easily capable of 70 mph. The rules did not allow the use of special racing parts but the Canadians were well aware of all the hotrodding tricks of the day. Stan Reynolds of Wetaskiwin had one of the faster cars and his modifications included a downdraft carburetor, ported intake manifold, a shaved head and a homemade racing cam. At least one racer, Tom Villetard, babbited the connecting rods off center to get more compression.

Model T action at Edmonton in 1948. Tom Villetard is leading in #23 with Stan Reynolds on the outside in #6.

Stan Reynolds' #5 Model T lies upside down on the track at Calgary in 1942. Reynolds was knocked unconscious and is receiving first aid at the right.

A Hudson sedan paces a field of stripped Model Ts at Calgary in 1949. Stan Reynolds is on the pole.

With speeds approaching 70 mph the Model T racing looked dangerous, and it was. The fragile Ts often broke wheels, spindles and axles. Crashes were frequent and so were injuries. There was only one fatality. This was Canadian serviceman Corporal G. Segar at Calgary on September 3, 1943.

There were many different winners in the Alberta T races, but three names stand out. Tom Villetard of Edmonton was a winner in the late 1940s. Stan Reynolds won more than his share of races. Another winner was Gordon Rasmussen of Strathmore—was he a relative of Indy racer Eldon Rasmussen?

After the war there were races at other Alberta towns, but by about 1948 the crowds started to drop off. There was competition from other racing and the support of wartime charities was no longer there. The final Model T races were held in Calgary in 1951 before a crowd of only 2,000. Thus ended one of the most remarkable and little known eras in racing history.

Information for this chapter came from the booklet, *Roaring Lizzies: Model T Ford Racing in Alberta, 1941 to 1951,* by Kelly Busick. Also thanks to Stan Reynolds, President of the Reynolds Museum in Wetaskiwin, Alberta. All photos are from Stan's collection.

Arkansas

It is unlikely that there was any pre-World War II roadster racing in Arkansas. There were limited amounts of midget and big car racing but the roadsters did not get started until about 1946.

There were a few nice looking roadsters built in Arkansas but most of the cars that raced were primitive beyond belief. The racing started at Devils Bowl in Hot Springs where the events were billed as the "Junk Yard Derby." An unflattering name but aptly descriptive. It appears that coupes were allowed to run at first but soon it was all open cars—VERY open cars! It seems that the first step to building a car to race at Hot Springs was to remove the body completely. Most of the cars had rollbars but few bothered with a firewall.

Two cars tangle at Devils Bowl. For sure, there was no cutting into the infield on this turn!

Edd Foshee at Spa. Had McDonald's existed then Foshee, with that rollbar, was a natural for some big bucks "Golden Arches" sponsorship.

At some point in 1947 another track was built in Hot Springs—Spa Speedway. While Devils Bowl had been a semi off-road track, Spa was a nice looking oval. Here the cars were billed as hot rods and at least a few of the cars were comparable to roadsters racing in other parts of the country at that time. That same year there was night racing at a midget track in Benton. Ray Shillito won most of the races, but Paul Swindle, Jack Crabtree and Steve Mangus were also top drivers.

It is probable that roadster races (or some form thereof) were held in other Arkansas cities but nothing definite showed up in research. It is certain that there were not very many Arkansas roadsters. Stock car racing very quickly replaced the hot rods in Arkansas. Information on the purses is almost nonexistent. The only notation is from a news clipping that mentions, "A crowd of less than 200 braved the chill winds of the Devils Bowl yesterday." The article goes on to say that Jack Crabtree won the $100 purse. Looks like it was winner take all and that the promoter took a bath that day. Despite the unsafe looking cars there were no known roadster fatalities in Arkansas and, apparently, no serious injuries.

Most of the information and all of the photos for the Arkansas chapter came from Sonny Shillito of Hot Springs. Sonny's dad, Ray, did well in the roadsters and went on to a long and very successful career in modified stock car racing.

This is Rush Simpson at Devils Bowl in Hot Springs. Check the firewall and the location of the fuel tank—not to worry, surely he's running a fuel tank bladder!

Ray Shillito is in #11 at Benton in 1947. Shillito later did very well in the stocks and modifieds—we can assume that he bought a helmet!

Action at Devils Bowl in 1947. Ray Shillito leads sans helmet and goggles.

Devils Bowl. Car #98 is not a bad looking roadster, but nothing is known about it.

The caption on this photo read "Ray Shillito and his hot rod. From that front bumper Devils Bowl racing must have been a contact sport.

1946 and probably at Devils Bowl in Hot Springs. Ray Shillito on the inside races with an unidentified sedan. Closed cars were soon banned.

This is "Shine and his hot rod". Primitive, but Shine is running dual carbs.

Sam White in action at Spa Speedway in Hot Springs.

Arizona

Roadster racing in Arizona can, in general, be divided into two parts. This would be the racing with local cars, that probably started in 1936 at Holbrook and that, that continued at various tracks throughout the roadster era. There were a couple of Arizona roadster organizations formed, but the names of these groups have been forgotten. Most of the other racing in Arizona was that sanctioned by the Los Angeles area-based California Roadster Association.

After World War II roadster races in Arizona were held at Holbrook. These were strictly for Arizona cars—they were usually billed as "hot rods," but most were primitive machines not far removed from the jalopy stage. Purses at Holbrook must have been very small—one 1949 news account mentions that "nearly 500 fans" witnessed the races. Allowing for a bit of exaggeration, and doing some arithmetic, the purse was surely less than $100. It appears that Arizona cars tried racing in Phoenix, but the races were less than successful. An ad for a 1950 California Roadster Association event at South Mountain Speedway emphasizes that "These roadsters are RACE CARS—not hot rods."

Another unsuccessful Arizona promotion took place at Kinsley Ranch, south of Tucson, in 1948 when races were held on a newly constructed three-quarter-mile dirt oval. It was a hot day and no matter how much water was poured on the track, the dust was awful. Jimmy Bryan won the main event, but, sadly, there were two fatalities and that ended roadster racing at Kinsley Ranch.

Lee Sorrells at the wheel of a very nice-looking Arizona car. The engine is a 248 cubic inch Buick eight and the body is from a DeSoto. Although essentially a street rod, the car won a lot of Arizona races. (Bonnie Sorrells Collection)

There were some good roadsters built in Arizona, but most of the cars remained rather crude. There was also a chronic car shortage and it appears that most of the races in the Phoenix area were dual-shows with the midgets. During this same period

PHOENIX SPEEDWAY

In the late summer of 1947 there were a series of roadster races held at Phoenix Speedway. Phoenix Speedway? Certainly a track with a name like this would be an important part of the rich racing history of this Arizona city. Well—yes and no. Phoenix Speedway, located at 62nd Street and East Thomas Road, has been all but forgotten. Allan Brown's fine book, *The History of America's Speedways—Past and Present,* lists 17 racetracks in Phoenix, but Phoenix Speedway is not among them. Brown lists a Thomas Road Speedway and only through some fine detective work by racing historian, Bill Hill, was it learned that this was once called Phoenix Speedway.

At least three apparently successful hot rod races were held at Phoenix Speedway. Among the drivers competing were future Indy racers Bobby Ball and Jimmy Bryan. The sanctioning body for the races if any is unknown, but most of the cars came from a California group called the Gate City Racing Association (GCRA). Press clippings indicated this group was based in one of the southern California cities of Compton, Pomona or maybe San Bernardino. In 1947 the California Roadster Association (CRA) dominated southern California hot rod racing and kept busy five to six nights a week. Apparently the GCRA was picking up some of the leftovers and racing at places like Oceanside, Downey, San Bernardino and Pomona. The group's top driver was "The Colton Flash", Ray Smith. For the most part this group avoided being "found" in five years of roadster racing research. Ray Smith appears only in Phoenix Speedway publicity—sorry, Ray!

This is the program cover for August 2, 1947 at the Phoenix Speedway. Car #81 is future Indy driver Bobby Ball. (Bill Hill Collection)

The photo on the cover of the Phoenix Speedway program indicates that the track was located at a baseball park. The clippings do mention a "one-fifth mile oval" which was the norm for ballparks. Midget races had been run there and Jimmy Bryan and Bobby Ball were among the drivers. Such a track is hardly ideal for roadsters, but if press clippings can be believed the races were excellent and drew good crowds. Main event winners for the three races that can be documented by newspaper clippings were Jimmy Bryan, Ray Smith and Bobby Ball. Ball won a 75 lapper that carried the title of "Arizona Hot Rod King."

As previously mentioned the California-based Gate City group supplied the bulk of the cars for the Phoenix Speedway hot rod races. This meant a tow of over 300 miles for these cars. It is not known what happened to the Phoenix Speedway racing after these three races, but at some point the term "hot rod" must have left a bad taste in the fans mouths. Note the March 25, 1950 ad for the CRA ROADSTER races.

An interesting side note to the Phoenix Speedway clippings is that Jimmy Bryan had somehow acquired the nickname "Lover Boy" Ten or so years later would you like to have walked up to the big, tough, cigar smoking, Arizona Cowboy and said, "Hi, Lover Boy!" Thanks to Rocky Rockwell of Chandler, Arizona for most of the information in this sidebar.

---

there were frequent "invasions" by the California Roadster Association. These races, at several tracks, were better organized and included three 100-mile races on the one-mile dirt oval at the Arizona State Fairgrounds in Phoenix. Some of the better Arizona cars competed in these races and came home winners in 1950 and 1956.

Information in the first roadster-racing history book, *Roaring Roadsters,* indicated that roadster racing in Arizona, as in most of the nation, was over by about 1956. Not so—make that 1971! Arizona roadster racing wasn't dead in 1956, it was merely on vacation.

The "modern" era of roadster racing began in 1961 at Tucson Speedway. A group called the Tucson Auto and Cycle Racing Association (TACRA) had been formed in 1948 for the purpose of racing stock cars. By the 1960s the organization had evolved into a modified-coupe-racing group, but fan interest was dwindling and crowds were down. Most of the cars

South Mountain Speedway in Phoenix in about 1952. Harry Stockman is on the pole in the C and T Automotive Merc as Don O'Riley (aka Don Urgo) battles on the outside. (Jim Ruth Collection)

Jim Ruth leads an unidentified roadster at Phoenix during the 1956 sprint-roadster 100 mile race. Note that the hood is flopping lose on #9—the rough track took a heavy toll on cars that day. (Jim Ruth Collection)

Al King spins out at Prescott in 1947 as Gene Gunn just misses. Gunn's #6 is powered by the combination popular with the very early hot rodders—A '28 Chevy with an Olds three-port head. (Bonnie Sorrells Collection)

were '32 to '34 Ford coupes with Chevy V8 engines. Nobody knows where the idea came from, but somebody suggested that the tops be cut off the cars. "It will be better if the fans can see the drivers." Out came the cutting torches and, presto, roadster racing was reborn in Arizona.

The cars differed a bit from earlier track roadsters in that stock Ford frames had to be used. Engines were almost all Chevy V8s and were limited to 325 cubic inches. "Roadster type" bodies were required, so It wasn't long before the heavy '32 to '34 bodies came off and were replaced by Model T or gutted Model A bodies. Rollbars were apparently required, though most were but a single hoop and provided little protection for the driver.

The reborn roadsters raced, mostly at Tucson Speedway, from 1961 until 1968. In 1969 the cars were called "Modifieds" and had cage rollbars, but for the most part, the roadster bodies were used and they still looked like track roadsters. This form of roadster racing went on until the early 1970s and was definitely (I think!) the last roadster racing in the United States.

Drivers who starred in the Tucson races included RC Whitwell, who won several championships, Jerry Miller, Bud Lee and Ollie Horton. There was also a "fine young driver" who is still winning races — Leland McSpadden! Purses for the races were not large—R.C. Whitwell recalls that winning a main-event seldom paid over $50.

A typical Holbrook car in about 1948. Holbrook did have two classes of cars—jalopies and hot rods, but by main event time the car count was usually low and all cars ran together. (Bob Noe Collection)

Kinsley Ranch near Tucson in March of 1948. It is not known who drove #66, but it could have been one of three drivers who were in that race and later made it to Indy—Jimmy Bryan, Bill Cheeseburg or Roger McCluskey. (Roy Eaton Collection)

This could be Bobby Ball at Kinsley Ranch, but it is probably Charlie Montgomery. The body of the car was later completed following the "graceful" lines of the cowl and it was known as the "Boxcar." (Roy Eaton Collection)

It is 1964 and the roadsters roar again in Tucson! (RC Whitwell Collection)

This is the completed "Boxcar" with Charlie Montgomery at the wheel. The car, powered by a Chrysler Six, was a lot faster than it looked and would have won a New Mexico roadster championship had anybody bothered to record points. (Bob Noe Collection)

A 1966 program cover at Tucson—not unlike 1946! (RC Whitwell Collection)

A mixed field of roadsters and sprint cars gets ready to qualify for a hundred-miler on the one-mile Phoenix oval. (Jim Ruth Collection)

March 25, 1950 and the advertising writer strives to undo the apparent poor reputation of the "hot rods." These must have been local cars that previously put on a poor show. (Bill Hill Collection)

RC Whitwell won a lot of races at Tucson in this Chevy V8 powered roadster. Although it looks heavy the body is gutted so that it weighs only about 100 pounds. (RC Whitwell Collection.)

Heavy traffic in a 1964 Tucson roadster race. This photo is from the track program. (RC Whitwell Collection)

Car No. 1 Driver ... Date ...

Check To

	Position	Earnings		Points
Time Trials	1	6	–	10
Trophy Dash	2	2	–	3
Heats	2	4	–	4
Main	1	34	–	50
Other				
Day's Totals		46	-	67
Previous Totals		175	35	265
Totals to Date		221	35	332

Here is RC Whitwell's payoff stub for May 22, 1965. He couldn't have done much better than this yet the payoff was only $46—it is estimated that the total purse that night was $200. (RC Whitwell Collection)

Dust billows up from behind a car at Kinsley Ranch. Eugene Gasser was killed in dusty, four-car pileup during this race. In a separate accident a spectator was killed by a loose wheel. (Roy Eaton Collection)

British Columbia

BY BRIAN PRATT

The geography of western British Columbia pretty well divided the roadster racing history of the province into two parts. There was racing on the mainland in the Vancouver area and on Vancouver Island in and around the city of Victoria. To get from one area to the other requires an expensive ferryboat trip.

Racing began near Victoria in 1934 on a mile horse track at Colwood and continued at The Willows Fairgrounds in 1935. Some of the competing cars can be classified as track roadsters. The sanctioning body, the British Columbia Automotive Sports Association (BCASA) did not permit cars with any special racing equipment other than pistons.

The Jack Smith car of 1935 was a 1921 four cylinder Olds with White truck pistons, Packard rods, two 1917 Hudson side draft carburetors and a home ground cam. Phil Foster, Johnny Wright, Bill

Promoter and track owner Andy Digney is shown with one of the very nice looking Washington Roadsters. The driver is Phil Foubert and he won several main events at Digney. (Digney Collection)

This is Colwood Park in Victoria in 1934. On the pole is George Lapp in what is definitely a track roadster. (McMurtry Collection)

Action in what newspaper reports called a "Tin Lizzie " race at Langford in 1947. They look like fairly fast cars. (Victoria Auto Racing Hall of Fame)

Pearson, Jimmy Laird and George Lapp, amongst others, were also involved in those formative years leading up to the beginning of big car racing at Langford Speedway in 1938.

There was one "bug" race run as part of a big car show at Langford before the war. "Bugs" were amalgamations of various car parts that many Victoria kids put together for road vehicles. They definitely could be considered hot rods although the 1930s depression precluded much "souping up" of engines.

On the mainland prewar jalopy races were held in 1941 in Vancouver at Con Jones Park as part of the midget race programs. Cars (almost certainly roadsters and stripped down) were to be earlier than 1928. Vancouver midget racing pioneer Walt Armstrong was involved and Sammy Snell won one race with his "Oakland Special" but most of this form of racing is lost in the dusty haze of dirt track history.

After the war, in 1946 and 1947, there were Model T races held at The Willows Fairground in Victoria and a few exhibitions at Langford Speedway in Vancouver. It appears that the stripped down cars were stock and that little, if any, cheating went on so perhaps these were not really roadster races.

Another view of the cars at Colwood Park in 1934. Phil Foster in #1 is driving a modified Chevy roadster. Ed Allen's #3 is a bobtail. (McMurtry Collection)

Larry Miller in #8 and Frank Kratzer in #11 run close together at Digney in 1950. This is probably a posed publicity shot. (Kratzer Collection)

Andy Digney in Burnaby, near Vancouver, built Digney Speedway in 1948. The quarter mile paved oval opened with midgets that were mostly from the Seattle area. A few roadster programs were held with American cars and Len Sutton won a couple of main events. They again provided shows in 1949 when Digney and the local midgets temporarily parted ways.

Lee Kirk of Yakima was involved in a spectacular crash at Digney in 1949 when he went flipping over the wall and hit the ticket office. The ticket office was vacant, though normally manned by Mrs. Digney. Racing could have come to an abrupt end in Burnaby if she had been in the office.

In late 1949 a serious attempt was made to race Canadian cars at Digney Speedway. This began when the formation of the British Columbia Roadster Racing Association (BCRRA) was announced in the Vancouver News-Herald on August 17, 1949. The idea for the club, and another similar one formed in

Victoria in 1950, seems to have come about from a meeting of promoters Andy Digney, and Bruce Passmore of Langford Speedway in Victoria. Both wanted to feature local cars to cut the costs of bringing in American cars. Altruism came in the form of wanting to rid the streets of the "hot rod Scourge."

The 1950 season saw the BCRRA sharing the bill at Digney Speedway with the British Columbia Midget Auto Racing Association in an attempt to have an all-local program. Andy Digney planned an ambitious season of Wednesday and Saturday night racing. Frank Kratzer won the opening night race on May 27, 1950.

Larry McBride was the dominant roadster driver. At one point of the season he was awarded a trophy for having won the trophy dash three successive times and, although it wasn't announced officially, he won the points championship. Other main event winners during the year were Larry Miller, Johnny Gottselig and Dave Clark. Unfortunately the payoff

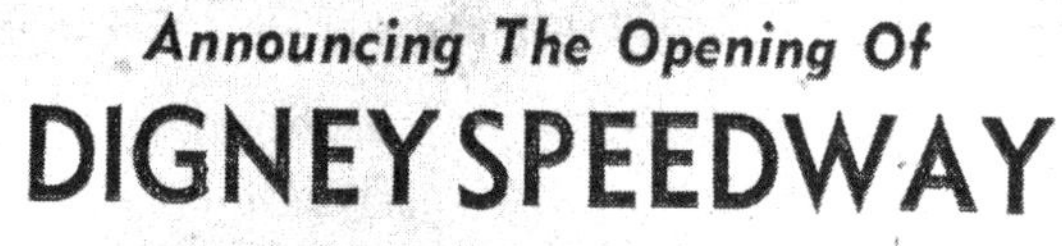

A 1950 ad for Digney Speedway. Even with both the midgets and roadsters racing (in separate events) the fields were short. (Digney Collection)

This is a 1951 ad for Digney Speedway near Vancouver. Very few Canadian cars competed with the Washington roadsters (Digney Collection)

POSSIBLE ILLEGAL ACTIVITIES?

Canada has some very high import fees on many items—this includes racing parts. The import fee, along with an unfavorable exchange rate, made getting US made racing parts very expensive for Canadian racers. In the past few years I've heard some great stories of how attempts were made to sneak racing parts into Canada. I thought that perhaps some of the roadster racers were involved in what seems a bit of a sport to the Canadians. I asked Brian Pratt about this and here is his reply. Names have been changed to protect the possibly not so innocent.

"As far as a sidebar on high Canadian import fees and smuggling I can't say that I have any roadster related stories. Most of what I know comes from the Langford big cars.

"Probably this is so because the roadsters in B.C. didn't get a chance to develop like the big cars did and make the contacts that the guys in Victoria did in Seattle.

"Sam Smith told me he once took his race car down to the US with a beat up old engine in it and got a brand new one installed. At the border coming back he told the customs official they'd had bad luck at the races and the official said better luck next time. And Canada had another racing engine. At US prices.

"And, of course, Joe Jones would fly in from the US to race at Langford. He'd log a flight a little longer than necessary so that he could land twice in the Victoria area. Once to offload some parts and the second time at the scheduled time of arrival. Sam Smith was quick to point out that he was often at the first landing scene.

"Booze was a popular smuggling item. Racers from the US were often encouraged to put a bottle of fine, cheap liquor in those straight pipes of the big cars.

"So I have stories but nothing really relating to track roadsters. I just don't think the Vancouver lads, or the younger Victoria guys, had the contacts developed. If they had been given a few more years I'm sure the smuggling would have included fond memories"

Frank Kratzer gets some advice from Ray McBride before a Digney race. (Kratzer Collection)

This photo appeared in the Vancouver Sun in 1950. Publicity for the roadsters was quite good. (Digney Collection)

Larry McBride in 1950. With the heavy Model A body McBride couldn't be expected to compete with the Washington roadsters but he was the class of the field among local cars. (McBride Collection)

system left lots to be desired, mostly in the lack of bucks.

The BCRRA just did not have enough cars and the midgets weren't doing much better. One Wednesday night show was canceled when only five midgets and four roadsters appeared. Digney was forced back to a weekly show and he once again began bringing the roadsters from Washington to guarantee a full field.

In 1951 a handful of roadster races, sanctioned by the Roadster Racing Association of Washington (RRAW), were held at Digney. By then the Washington group was also short of cars and one Digney race had to be canceled when eight cars were crashed at Aurora Stadium the previous night.

One problem for Andy Digney was to bring an American racecar into British Columbia a bond had to be posted with Canadian Customs. Even with Digney and the RRAW handling the paperwork it wasn't always smooth sailing across the border.

The last mention of the BCRRA is the building of a dirt track in Langley, 30 miles east of Vancouver, in 1954. The track was probably Wonderland Speedway, which didn't last, and if there was a roadster race on it, it was never recorded.

Local hot rods get ready for a race at Digney Speedway in 1950. Larry Miller is in #8, Larry McBride in #10 and at the far right is Frank Kratzer. (Digney Collection)

In Victoria the Vancouver Island Track Roadster Association (VITRA) was formed in 1950 with Les Webb as president. Their idea was to keep cars street legal and stock.

Les Webb remembers the first race at Langford

The "Tin Lizzies" parade as publicity for a 1947 race at The Willows in Victoria. It was implied that the cars were to be stock Ts but who knows for sure? (Victoria Auto Racing Hall of Fame)

A newspaper photo of a "Tin Lizzie" at The Willows in 1947. This was thought to be a Model T race but no way is #1 a T! (Victoria Auto Racing Hall of Fame)

late in 1950 when the roadsters were driven to the track, the headlights and windshields taped and the cars raced. Afterward the tape was removed and the roadsters driven home. By December the club had 52 members.

An article in a Victoria paper featured an Oldsmobile, a '35 Ford V8, Jack Smith created '29 Chevy with a Ford Six and a real oddball—a car made with parts from a Harvard trainer aircraft.

Unfortunately Langford Speedway closed at the end of the 1950 season and Victoria drivers were without a racetrack. In 1952 Shearing Speedway, in Duncan, north of Victoria over a mountain pass, opened. VITRA was the sanctioning body but the cars were "modified stock" and only a few were track roadsters.

Note: Brian Pratt is a racing historian living in Burnaby, British Columbia. His research has uncovered some remarkable information on British Columbia racing dating back to 1907. Many well-known American drivers competed in the races and some Canadian drivers later became big names in this country. Brian is in the early stages of a book on British Columbia racing history.

When the Vancouver Island Track Roadster Racing Association got started the emphasis was that street legal cars would be racing. It looks like the publicity was very good as this series of photos was published in the Victoria Daily Times in September of 1950. (Victoria Auto Racing Hall of Fame Collection)

Central California

Geography pretty well divides central California into two areas—the San Joaquin Valley and the coastal section. Roadster racing was roughly divided the same way.

On the coast a form of roadster racing began very early. This was in Lompoc where annual street-road races were held from 1912 to 1917. The rules allowed cars up to 235 cubic inches to be entered but local resident Monte Huyck entered a car that can best be described as a hot rod. His Model T roadster was stripped of unnecessary parts and the engine, built by the Lompoc Ford dealer, was described as having "untold improvements". During the years that the races were run Huyck dominated and won over fields that included other Model Ts and heavier and more expensive cars. Huyck had payoffs up to $600. The State of California outlawed road racing in 1918 but Huyck continued to campaign Model T powered racers on dirt tracks in the Lompoc-Santa Maria area. One has to wonder if Monte Huyck had something to do with the interest in Model T racing that remained high in the area for several decades.

In about 1936 the Lompoc Model T Club was formed and this group held what can best be described as an off road race that wound through the surrounding countryside. The Ts also used public roads and, technically, this must have been against the law. A few years later the T Club started to hold races on oval tracks. The rules are a bit vague and may have changed over the years but there appears to have been a stock and a modified class for T roadsters. The modified cars slowly evolved into true track roadsters. Some literature indicates that in the modified class anything was OK as long as it was a flathead. Other data implies that overheads were permitted. The Lompoc T Club enjoyed the support of the community and the races went on at several different tracks until about 1950. By then most of the

This is about 1912 at the Surf-Oceanside Track west of Lompoc. Monte Huyck is leading in a very early version of a track roadster. (Lompoc Historical Society Collection)

Monte Huyck roars through downtown Lompoc during the street-road race on July 4, 1914. Huyck turned the fastest lap at an average speed of 54.3 MPH. (Lompoc Historical Society Collection)

A news clipping for the 1915 Lompoc race which Monte Huyck won. Myra Manfrina and Dave Cole of the Lompoc Historical Society provided the photos and information on the Lompoc street-road races.

Monte Huyck (left) and riding mechanic Allen Arkley get ready for the 1916 Lompoc 100-mile race. Sponsor Pinal-Dome Refining Company supplied the snazzy driving uniforms. (Lompoc Historical Society Collection)

After street-road racing was outlawed in California in 1918 Monte Huyck took to the oval dirt tracks in his hot Model T. This photo was probably taken at Santa Maria. (Coast Auto Racing—Bob Garner Collection)

An unidentified member of the Lompoc Model T Club poses alongside of his racer at the Maretti Track near Surf. (Lompoc Historical Society Collection)

Ts were gone and the club sanctioned or sponsored roadster races with cars from the Porterville and Los Angeles areas.

In California's Central Valley roadster racing probably started in 1933 when poorly organized races were held in farmers' fields. In 1934 the San Joaquin Valley Racing Association was formed. It is unclear how many races this outfit held but Bryce Morris was crowned champion with 372 points. A 1934 news clipping mentions that promoter Charlie Curryer put on 25 roadster races in the San Joaquin valley that year. Morris' point total doesn't sound like 25 races so perhaps Curryer promoted another group? In 1935 an Owners and Drivers Association is listed as sanctioning races at Modesto and other tracks. The roadsters were obviously very active at a number of tracks in the area in 1934 and 1935. From 1936 until after World War II there is almost no evidence of roadster racing in the San Joaquin Valley. There was at least one race held at Madera but this was with cars that were mostly from the San Francisco area. It is not known what happened to the seemingly active San Joaquin Valley roadster program.

Most of the postwar racing in this area was at Porterville where the Central Valley Racing Association (CVRA) sanctioned the roadsters. The group was small, but active, and enjoyed the support of local merchants and fans. For the most part the roadster fields were small with mostly local cars but special races did attract larger fields with visitors from other areas. The purses for these special races weren't bad but on an average night at Porterville the purse could be as low as $100.

During the late 1940s and early '50s the midgets were very strong in the San Joaquin Valley so this could account for the fact that there wasn't too much roadster racing. The Los Angeles based California Roadster Association (CRA) held a few races at Bakersfield and at Fresno's Airport Speedway.

Gene Pernu won some early Porterville races in this neat A-V8. (Tommy Morrow Collection)

Paul Clapper won the dash at Buellton in the Andy Boydston Merc. Here he gets his trophy from a pretty young miss. (Paul Clapper Collection)

This is the aftermath of Scotty Cain's sensational fence busting episode at Porterville. It seems impossible, but Cain walked away with only minor injuries. (Bagnall Collection)

The start of a Lompoc Model T Club race in 1948. The modified Ts could hit over 70 MPH on the half-mile Rodeo Grounds oval. (Lompoc Historical Society)

May 1940 and a field of Lompoc T Club racers get set for an event at the Maretti Track. The oval was only a few miles from the Pacific Ocean and must have been nearly pure sand. (Lompoc Historical Society Collection)

The Howard Cams Merc has just won the main event at the Santa Maria Fairgrounds. The driver is unknown.

The California Roadster Association from the Los Angeles area visited the Santa Maria Fairgrounds in about 1950.

Opening of Season For

San Joaquin Valley Roadster Racing

NEWMAN, Calif.—SUNDAY, APRIL 21
10-Lap Heat Races — 30-Lap Final—Half-Mile Track
$100.00 GUARANTEED PURSE

CHOWCHILLA, Calif.—SUNDAY, MAY 5
100 MILER (Mile Speedway)
$200.00 Guaranteed Purse

Trophy Dashes at Each Event—For Valley Championship

OTHER DATES TO FOLLOW

Write for Entry Blanks
SAN JOAQUIN VALLEY RACING ASSN.
or BOYLE VALVE RACING CLUB—2128 Hammond, Fresno, Calif

Roadster purses were a bit on the low side in 1935. During this period big car purses would be around $250 and the midgets a bit better. (Coast Auto Racing—Bob Garner Collection)

From the photo caption Morris may have competed against big cars in winning his championship. He later became a top midget driver. (Coast Auto Racing—Bob Garner Collection)

Bryce Morris built and drove this nice looking modified roadster at Chowchilla in 1932. That's Bryce next to the blonde at the left. Morris soon switched to the midgets but kept the blonde. (Trueblood Collection)

Early roadster action at Porterville. No identification on the drivers of what appears to be street rods. (Tommy Morrow Collection)

In 1952 the Lompoc T Club was a Model T organization in name only. Here is Paul Clapper of Porterville lined up for a race at the club's track in Buellton. (Paul Clapper Collection)

Dick Meyer wins a dash in the Bob Phipps Alexander Overhead valve V8. The trophy girl is Kay Clapper, wife of racer Paul Clapper. (Paul Clapper Collection)

This is 1948 and the T Club was racing at the Rodeo Grounds in Lompoc. Looks like there is a flathead in this cutdown T. (Lompoc Historical Society Collection)

THE BATHTUB

All roadster racing organizations had rules that required roadster bodies and odds are that the CVRA had the same rule. Obviously this didn't stop Les Cone from racing his "Bathtub" for a couple of years. It is known that Cone used a potent flathead Model B Ford engine but the chassis make is unknown. So is the make of that touring car body. The car appears heavy, and probably was, but Cone did OK and even chalked up a main event win.

Les Cone destroyed the car in a violent flip in 1950. He was not seriously injured but did not drive again.

Les Cone is half out of the "Bathtub" as he flips at Porterville. (Al Gray Collection-Edwards Studio Photo)

The remains of the Les Cone "Bathtub" after his crash. The car was considered totaled and not rebuilt. (Paul Clapper Collection)

Robert Rupert takes a wild flip at Hanford in 1955. This was during the era when the California Roadster Association ran both sprints and the hot rods. Jack Rounds is in the sprint car. (Bagnall Collection)

Rosie Roussel gets another trophy at Porterville. Car #4 is the Miller Crankshaft Special from Los Angeles. (Rosie Roussel Collection)

Bob Bartlett gets a trophy from a very young Porterville lady. (Bob Bartlett Collection)

Prentice Knudsen wrecked his Pontiac at Porterville. The six-cylinder engine performed well against the Mercs. (Edwards Studio Photo—Paul Clapper Collection)

Heavy traffic at Porterville in 1950. Car #61 is Jack Rook with Dick Chartrand in #56 and Sam Judy in #5. (Edwards Studio Photo—Al Gray Collection)

Dick Meyer wrecked this roadster at Porterville. Meyer had great talent and was totally fearless—a trait that may have contributed to his death in a 100-MPH highway crash. (Edwards Studio Photo—Paul Clapper Collection)

Jim Bonding cranks out a fast lap as the California Roadster Association visits Fresno's Airport Speedway in 1949. (Tommy Morrow Collection)

Future midget ace, Tommy Morrow, started his career in this less than sleek rear engined car. Morrow remembers that it handled about like it looked and that "something always broke." (Tommy Morrow Collection)

So far as is known the CRA ran only once at Airport Speedway in Fresno. Wonder why? (Tommy Morrow Collection)

Paul Clapper in an ex-dry lakes Oldsmobile Eight. The frame of this car is supposed to be from a c 1933 Indy Miller. (Paul Clapper Collection)

Colorado

Roadster racing in Colorado began in the early 1930s at the Dupont Speedway near Denver. The five-eighths mile Dupont Speedway was one of the few paved ovals so the racers there enjoyed the luxury of not having to fight dust. The Dupont cars were probably a mixture of street roadsters and cars that were built specifically for racing. There are records of a few Ford V8s racing at Dupont—a rarity in prewar racing. There was almost certainly roadster racing at other Colorado tracks but no information is available.

After World War II a few rather disorganized races were held before the Colorado Auto Racing Club (CARC) was formed in late 1946. The first races were held in Littleton at the Arapahoe County Fairgrounds and attracted capacity crowds. Only a flimsy wire fence separated the spectators from the racecars and it is a miracle that a major disaster did not take place. In mid-1947 most of the hot rod racing moved to Englewood Speedway—a fine midget track in Denver. The CARC raced at other tracks in the Denver area and made several trips to Kansas, Nebraska and South Dakota. They also continued to tempt fate at the Arapahoe Fairgrounds as late as 1949.

Englewood Speedway was definitely the CARC home track and they put on some very good shows there. Information on the purses is sparse but the payoffs must have been good. There was no shortage of well-built and nice appearing cars. The CARC roadsters may have lacked some of the racing refinements of other areas but photos, almost without exception, show nicely painted and upholstered cars. Showmanship was important and the man behind this was probably Lafe Ellsworth who was president of the group during most of the roadster era. Typical of Ellsworth's leadership were having professional models serve as trophy girls.

The CARC roadsters served as a training ground for some very good race drivers. Keith Andrews was probably the most successful and had a couple of

Dupont Speedway on May 30, 1933. Perhaps #5 was in an exhibition roadster race at this big car event? This could have been the beginning of roadster racing in Colorado. (Stan Lee Collection)

Harry Yost gets a push from Willy Young at Englewood in 1946. Yost had broken an oil line and could not keep his very slippery foot on the throttle. (Yost Collection)

Harry Yost comes very close to stout looking post at the Arapahoe County Fairgrounds in Littleton. Dick Isaac is on the outside and Keith Andrews follows in #2. (Yost Collection)

Fred Massey in the Harvey Wilson V8 gets a trophy at Brighton. Note the minimal protection for spectators. (Sonny Coleman Collection)

Action at Englewood in 1947. Car #49 is either Russ Forges or Bob Coy—no identification on #78.

Ray Dutton spins the Norman Vanderlip Chevy to avoid a competitor. The driver on the left sits high and exposed—would today's drivers race this machine?

starts at Indy before being killed at that track in 1957. Sonny Coleman used the hot rods as a beginning to a long and successful career in the midgets. Willy Young went on to become the driver of the 270-MPH Bonneville Kenz-Leslie streamliner.

Note the photos of the Denver cars and how different they all are. Denver racers must have been a rare breed of non-copycats!

Most of Colorado's population is centered in the Denver area and that's where most of the roadster racing was. In the southern part of the state the Durango Auto Racing Association was formed and ran a mixture of roadsters and home built sprint cars. This organization ran at Durango and Pagosa Springs in Colorado and several tracks in New Mexico and Arizona. Archie Bado of Durango built a Ford Six roadster that was quite successful. With New Mexico's Jay Abney at the wheel this car outraced and outlasted a 50-car field to win a road race at Agoura, California in 1952.

Unless otherwise noted all photos in the Colorado chapter are from the Leroy Byers Collection.

THE STUDEBAKER

One of the major errors in *Roaring Roadsters* concerns the Colorado chapter and the sidebar "An Indy Car Mystery". This related how it was probable that the Studebaker powered roadster that ran on Denver area tracks was an ex-Indy car. Some of the history of the car was known and it was a reasonable assumption—or so I thought!

It was too late to make any changes when I found Harry Syer who owned the Studebaker in the 1940s. He told me the true history of the car. While the Studebaker factory was very active at Indy in the early 1930s two-man era, the car Syer ran as a roadster was not one of the Indy cars. It was built as a one-man big car, either by or for Willard Prentiss, in about 1935. (Prentiss drove at Indy in 1933 and finished 13th in a Duesenberg) Prentiss raced the car at Legion Ascot with a Fronty T engine. At some point the car came to the Denver area and was owned by Bill Kenz. Harry and George Syer bought the car for $25 and installed a Galvin DOHC Model T engine. A year or so later the Syer brothers bought the Studebaker engine from Kenz for another $25.

Pappy Hendricks is shown in the Syer Studebaker in 1947. That should be Harry and George Syer with the car. (Leroy Byers Collection)

The history of that Studebaker engine remains partly a mystery. It is known that the eight-cylinder power plant was built by Bud and Ed Winfield and it appears to be an improved version of the Indianapolis engines. The block was lightened by aluminum side covers and it had a lighter crankshaft. With 336 cubic inches it put out 240 horsepower at 4000 RPM—more than the factory Indy engines. One would have to think that the engine was built for Indy—and that it was expensive. There were privately entered Studebakers at Indy until 1937—maybe this engine was in one of those cars. How it got to Denver is another missing piece of the puzzle.

The Syer brothers ran the Studebaker big car until it was badly wrecked at Belleville, Kansas in about 1940. When roadster racing started in 1946 they put a roadster body on it. With drivers like Pappy Hendricks and Keith Andrews at the wheel the car was a very successful track roadster. The big Stude put out a lot more horsepower than the predominately V8 competition and it would stay cool.

The Syer car had a very different appearance than most of the Colorado roadsters. The knockoff wire wheels gave it the look of an Indy car and Harry Syer remembers that it was often advertised as just that. I apologized to Syer about my error in representing the car as an actual Indy machine. Harry laughed and said something like, "Hell, I won't tell anybody."

Harry Yost started his driving career in this street A-V8. Harry's brother, Ed, is at the left with mechanic Cecil Vogel on the right. (Harry Yost Collection)

This car looks fresh off of the street. Scotty Johnson smiles for the cameraman at Brighton.

An exceptionally nice street rod at Brighton in 1946. The driver is unknown but Bill Agnew, second from left, was the owner.

Al "Porky" Laughlin was the owner-driver of this A V-8 at Englewood. The Denver photographers, Lynn Day and Leroy Byers, were thoughtful enough to include the hard working pitcrews in the photos,

Probably 1947 at Englewood. Howard Wolfe in #15 chases Red Fitzwater. Fitzwater was CARC champion in 1948 and 1949.

Gerald Rallens at Englewood in 1949. Those are probably "Denver Heads"—the Ford Motor Company's high altitude-high compression option.

Red Fitzwater in the Charlie Codner Merc gets a trophy from a pretty model.

The CARC seldom missed a chance to promote the hot rods. Hub Cook, left, and club president Lafe Ellsworth are with this exhibit at a sports show in Denver.

Future Indy driver Keith Andrews in a 1949 roadster ride. At left is owner Hub Cook with pitcrew Walt Schmidtz, Harold Gilbert and Paul Dives.

This should be John Kennedy at Englewood. That roadster body must be channeled a good 18-inches!

No ID on this car with the much modified body. Can anybody recognize that very stout frame?

ROADSTERS ON PIKES PEAK

The Pikes Peak Hillclimb is one of the most traditional events in US racing. Ever since 1916 men and machines have been challenged by the torturous climb up the 14,110-foot Colorado mountain. For many years the race was sanctioned by the American Automobile Association (AAA) and carried points that counted towards the national championship. Even though the event was classified as a "Championship" race, like Indianapolis, a remarkable number of roadsters took part. Possibly the almost chronic shortage of cars in the prewar years had something to do with the bending of the rules to allow roadsters to compete.

Some of the cars competing in the Pikes Peak Hillclimb in the 1920s may have been modified roadsters but the first documented record is in 1931. Walt Killinger ran his Model A roadster with an OHV engine and finished fifth—Art Martinson was right behind in his OHV Model A. Over the period of the next ten years a dozen or so roadsters ran in the race. Notable was Marty Keller's Cragar-A that ran several times and Bill Kenz's Reverse Cam Cragar-Model A. These cars finished as high as sixth for payoffs of a big, fat zero—all the money was up front at Pikes Peak in those days. There were also several supercharged Ford V8 roadsters than ran, but these cars were not too successful.

After WW II it was the Bill Grover Chevy Six track roadster that ran well on Pikes Peak. Apparently the rules were a bit more selective as the car ran up the mountain with a race car body on it. In 1948 Herb Byers drove this car and finished second to many time winner Al Rogers in an Offy. Byers collected $2300 for his finish. This car ran the Pikes Peak race until 1957. In 1955 there was a new chassis but the same track roadster Chevy Six was in place as Slim Roberts finished second. Roberts was third in 1956 and Danny Morgan finished seventh in 1957. After that the Chevy Six was "retired" to Colorado sprint car races.

Lloyd Axle on his way up Pikes Peak in 1934. The Marty Keller owned Model A has a Cragar OHV engine. Axle finished sixth. (Leroy Byers Collection)

Slim Roberts slides around a turn on his way to a second place finish at Pikes Peak. Even though this is 1955 the Bill Grover car still has a Chevy Six that was used in a Colorado roadster in the late 1940s. (Leroy Byers Collection)

Don Padia in a nice looking car. Padia was one of the CARC's top drivers.

Red Dutton is shown with owner John Sobella in this 1948 Englewood photo. Day races at Englewood were rare so it must be early in the season.

Slim Roberts lucks out as two lovely models present the trophy at Englewood in 1950. CARC rules obviously allowed body modifications—something that most groups did not permit.

This Chevy powered hot rod has lots of room for the engine but very little for the unidentified driver.

Don Clark with owner Johnny Brandimere. The Brandimere family is still active in Colorado racing and runs the Brandimere Speedway drag strip in Denver.

Jack Smith, at left, was probably the driver of #17. Must be a six-cylinder flathead of some kind.

Rocky LaFant drove this very low roadster. It is scarcely more than knee high.

THE BILL KENZ CRAGAR

Bill Kenz was a big name in Colorado racing and a master mechanic. He ran track roadsters from the 1930s to the 1940s and, later on built a 270-mph streamliner for Bonneville. One of his first accomplishments was the Reverse Cam Cragar.

The Cragar overhead valve conversion for the Model A or B engine was very popular but, in general, poorly designed. It was sold for installation on an engine with a minimum of effort and the maximum use of stock parts. It had the standard two intake and four exhaust ports and would not perform as well as some of the other OHV units available.

The field comes down for the starter's flag at Sterling in 1936. It is not known who won the race but Lloyd Axle, in the Kenz Reverse Cam Cragar roadster, was second. (Stan Lee Collection)

Bill Kenz came up with a way to fix the Cragar's shortcomings. With a bit of machine work he rebuilt the camshaft so that it could be installed backwards and the valve timing would reverse the intake and exhaust ports. With now four intake ports the engine put out a lot more power. It is believed that Kenz built two, or perhaps three, reverse cams.

In the 1930s Bill Kenz had the engine in a 1931 Model A Ford roadster. The car ran in roadster races, at Pikes Peak and on July 4, 1936 in a big car race at Sterling, Colorado. With Lloyd Axle at the wheel the car took a pair of second places in the main event in two days of racing.

Kenz sold the car around 1940 and it was raced in the Detroit area. After the war it returned to Colorado under the ownership of Bob Conrad. Dick Issac did most of the driving in Colorado roadster races but, tragically, was killed in the car. The car was junked after the crash and the engine disappeared but the Reverse Cam has survived all these years. It is in a '28 Model A roadster-pickup owned by Ted Mahoney of Victor, Montana.

Sterling on July 4, 1936. There is a lot of Colorado racing history in this photo. Bill Kenz is on the left, the driver is one of the state's finest, Lloyd Axle, and midget great, Roy Leslie is on the right. (Stan Lee Collection)

This is a Bill Kenz Reverse Cam Cragar engine today. It is in Ted Mahoney's street rod in Victor, Montana. The engine is a full race stroker—Mahoney built the intake manifold. (Ted Mahoney Photo)

Don Padia in the roadster takes on Lloyd Axle in a match race at Brighton. Axle was seldom beaten and this race was no exception.

Florida

In Florida the wide ocean beaches were the sites of attempts on the world land speed record from the 1920s until the mid 1930s. It was only natural that local racers would discover these wonderful places to race. So far as is known the first organized races took place in the late 1930s. The cars were hopped up roadsters that Floridians called "skeeters" or "cut-downs. The racing was at low tide, around barrels placed about a half mile apart, on beaches at places like Daytona, Fernandina and Jacksonville. Drivers such as Bill and Stanley Lee, Gene McCarl and Bill Snowden raced mostly just for the fun of it. The purses, if any, were very small.

In the 1930s there were races held on a brick and dirt oval at Camp Foster, an Army base, near Jacksonville. These might have been something akin to roadster racing. Fred Frame is reported to have won a race there on April 1, 1934 in his '33 Ford V8 roadster stock car over a field of cars "built especially for racing."

A group of St Augustine skeeters pose for the cameraman. Note that the skeeters are capable of carrying four passengers. Most of them were all-purpose beach vehicles and not strictly racecars. (Billy Lee Collection)

After World War II racing resumed on the beaches and, thanks to Buddy Herndon, some data is available on races held at St Augustine. These races were better organized and a St Augustine Race Drivers Association was formed. The beaches were roped off and an attempt was made to charge admission. This apparently wasn't too successful and Herndon remembers that on a good day the winner made $25. Bill and Stanley Lee won some of the St Augustine races but younger drivers like Turk

The skeeters parade before a race on the beach at St Augustine in 1946. Bill Lee is in #12 and odds are that he won the race. (Billy Lee Collection)

Adams, Gene McCarl and Buddy Herndon were also winners. Beach racing at St. Augustine went on until about 1954 with stock cars also being raced and gradually replacing the skeeters. There was also beach racing at Daytona and Emil Reutimann in his Chevy Six was hard to beat. (The Reutimann family is still very active in racing).

At the same time the beach racing was going on there was oval track racing on horse tracks and stock car ovals. Races were held at Jacksonville, Daytona, Cocoa, Melbourne, De Land, Tampa, Orlando, Gainesville, Pompano Beach and at Brunswick, Georgia. In 1949 roadster races were held on a military base at Opa-Locka near Miami. Some of the competing cars were beach skeeters but most were roadsters built for track racing. Drivers who competed in these races included Buddy Herndon, Gene McCarl, Piggy Bennett, Emil Reutimann, Hank Pollard, Bobby Malzahn, Rags Carter and, probably, the legendary Red Farmer.

NASCAR promoted what was meant to be a major roadster race in February of 1949. This was at Davie, near Fort Lauderdale, on an abandoned WW II airfield. The race, on a two-mile circular course, attracted only a few really good roadsters from other

This is Jacksonville in 1949. No identification on the driver. (Bill Chubbuck Collection)

A group of skeeter drivers in about 1946. Frequent winner, Bill Lee, is the second from the left on the front row. (Billy Lee Collection)

Pompano in about 1950. Hank Pollard drove this car that was built in Indiana. (Dee Powell Collection)

Dur Howe drove this Florida roadster. Howe had prewar experience in Iowa and later earned a NASCAR Modified Championship (Dee Powell Collection)

areas. Bob Flock won the 100 mile race over Jim Rathmann in Andy Granatelli's V8.

Stock car racing, starting with modified coupes, was strong in Florida during the roadster era. This is probably the main reason roadster racing never really developed in the state.

ABOUT SKEETERS

Track or street roadsters were called many things in different parts of the country but the term "skeeter" was pretty much restricted to Florida.

Tom Tumbelty in the family skeeter. Tumbelty drove an OHV V8 powered skeeter to a win in one of the last races held on the St Augustine beach. This was in 1956. (Tom Tumbelty Collection)

Skeeters were early versions of dune buggies. They were used as transportation on Florida beaches. Most were constructed from Ford chassis' stripped to near nothing. Some used parts of roadster bodies while others had crude bodies made from plywood. They were lightweight and, even with stock engines, were fast machines. The racing skeeters had modified engines but most were relatively mild by track racing standards. One St Augustine skeeter must have had a very good engine as it was clocked at 117 MPH.

Skeeters could also be called a Florida version of a street hot rod. At the time the skeeters were not required to have a motor vehicle license to run on the beaches. There was no speed limit so the beaches became the Florida equivalent of the California dry lakes. Actual speed trials were rare as it was simpler just to race around barrels—something that wouldn't have worked out too well on the dusty dry lakes. While perhaps not a true track roadster the skeeters have a unique place in roadster racing history.

Buddy Herndon stuffed a Ford V8 into a tiny Austin roadster. Looks like there was no room for a firewall. (Herndon Collection)

Gene McCarl in #8 and Buddy Herndon on the outside are shown in action at a sandy and rutted Florida track. (Herndon Collection)

Marion Edwards built his track roadster out of a '35 Ford Coupe. The photo is taken at Pompano in about 1950. (Dee Powell Collection)

Car #43 is smoking badly at St Augustine. Buddy Herndon stays out wide as Jimmy Horan drives blind in #44. (Bill Chubbuck Collection)

Jacksonville in 1949. Jimmy Rofond in a very nice looking roadster chases Buddy Herndon in #1. (Herndon Collection)

Buddy Herndon is shown with a trophy he won someplace in Florida. The poster advertises a race in honor of Paul Pappy—a roadster racer who died in a stock car crash. (Herndon Collection)

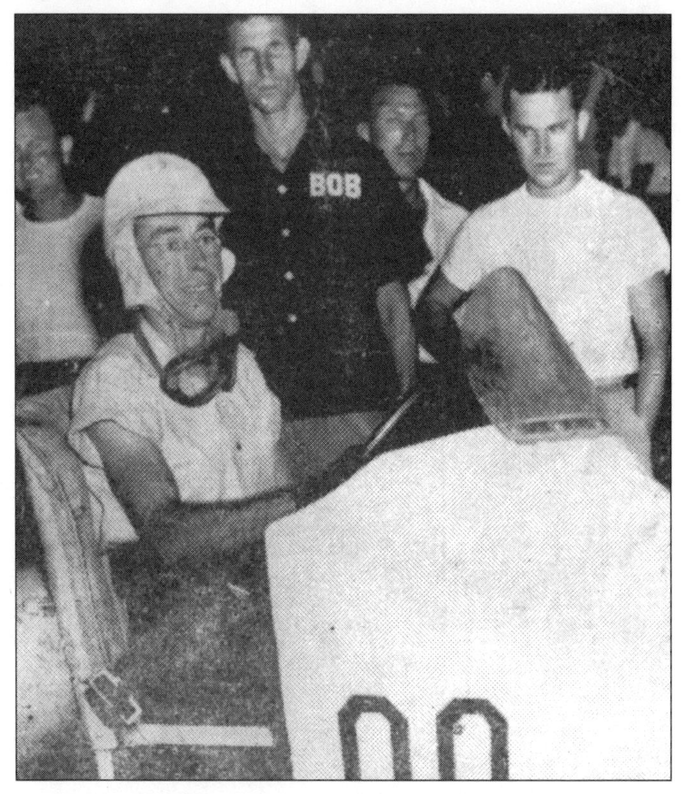

Emil Reutimann, patriarch of the racing Reutimann family, started his career in the roadsters. This photo is from a 1949 Gainesville program. (Herndon Collection)

This Florida hot rod looks like it was built from the remains of sprint car. No identification of owner or driver. (Herndon Collection)

Buddy Herndon incorporated a few modern sprint car ideas into his 1949 hot rod. Photo is at Cocoa. (Herndon Collection)

This is probably Speedway Park in Jacksonville. Buddy Herndon leads Gene McCarl. (Herndon Collection)

Gene McCarl was known as the "King of the Florida Hot Rods." Here he gets a trophy at St Augustine. (Jeannine Auth Collection)

This photo may have been taken at Orlando in 1949. The driver is Bud McBride of that city. (Herndon Collection)

Howard Mowell in action at Davie in the Lee Izor Chevy Six from Ohio. Mowell finished fourth in the hundred-miler on the two-mile circular course. (Izor Collection)

SOME FAMOUS GUYS

Some of the Florida roadster racers went on to become very good race drivers and did well in the sport. Al Powell with his box camera took these photos in 1948 at Opa-Locka near Miami.

Hank Pollard, Bobby Malzahn and Rags Carter raced in and won a lot of modified stock car races on the East Coast. Shorty Johns is the father of NASCAR star Bobby Johns—Bobby later drove this car. Red Farmer and Banjo Mathews certainly need no introduction.

All photos are from the Al [illegible]

[illegible]n

Roy Pressley is the drive [illegible] ***is Red Farmer talking to*** [illegible] ***folded).***

Shorty Johns

All of the cars in this 1949 action shot have "custom" bodies. (Herndon Collection)

It looks like Charlie Roberts did a fairly neat job of cutting down this '34 Ford Coupe body. (Dee Powell Collection)

Buddy Herndon used the front part of something and then built the rest of the body on his roadster. (Buddy Herndon Collection)

For some reason not many roadster style cars were sold in Florida. Maybe the tops rotted away in the wet climate? There was a definite shortage of roadster bodies for the Florida racers to use on their hot rods. Some of the bodies were built of sheet metal or even plywood. Other cars were built using cut down coupe bodies. Florida racing writer Marty Little remarks that "The neater builders used a torch to cut down the coupes—not an ax!"

Georgia

Georgia is stock car country and has been so for years. For an apparently brief period in the 1930s and the 1940s there was roadster racing. Thanks to Georgia racing historians, Mike Bell and Joe Cawley some information is available.

The roadster racing probably began at the Dan Bowles horse track at Augusta in the mid 1930s. Very little is known about these events. The name of Clyde Bullock is associated with this racing. Odds are the cars were called something akin to jalopy stock cars. In 1939 a similar form of racing took place in Macon.

In Savannah the first roadster race was held on January 1, 1947. Oddly enough this was the first postwar auto race in Savannah. Pre-race publicity promised "nationally known" drivers but "Cocoa, Fla. piston pusher Turk Adkins" was the only familiar name. The race sounds less than successful. Newspaper reports state "the races were (delayed) almost three hours due to weather conditions and other unavoidable delays." A scheduled "hell driver" act did not take place nor did a promised air show. Turk Adkins won the race in a hopped up '29 Model A. Another roadster race may or may not have taken place on June 4, 1947. Charles Zettrower, President of Jalopy Car Owners of America Inc, promoted both Savannah races.

The only other evidence of roadster racing in Georgia comes from the Savannah pre-race publicity. "Entries include Edsle Zettrower, driving a 1927 air-cooled Franklin, which he recently won first place with in a race at McRae"

It is certain that there is missing Georgia roadster racing information. It is equally certain that the roadsters really never got off the ground before the stock cars took over for good.

This rather fuzzy photo shows one of the cars that raced at Macon in 1939. It would be nice to think this is a construction photo but the car was probably raced this way. (Joe Cawley Collection)

Turk Adkins was billed as "Georgia Champion" in this Gainesville, Florida program photo. Seeing as how he won the only Georgia roadster race that can be documented he apparently earned the title. (Bob Fanning Collection)

Idaho

Roadster racing in Idaho began in the 1930s when Model T races were held at various Idaho county fairs. It is probable that most of these were a once a year event and that the cars were near to stock Ts. Calling this "track roadster" racing is pushing the definition a bit but there is no doubt most of the cars were roadsters.

Idaho has always been a bit remote so far as racing goes. It is not surprising that it took awhile for the roadsters in Idaho to become part of the post World War II boom. The Southern Idaho Racing Association (SIRA) was formed in 1951. It is unclear if the group was formed to race stock cars or roadsters but both types of cars ran in separate races at all events. There were only about ten track roadsters in the SIRA and, with an average of six or eight appearing at a race, there were just not enough cars to put on a full show. Races were held on horse tracks at Filer, Rupert, Jerome, Arco, Mackay, Pocatello and Twin Falls. In 1954 and 1955 races were held at a stock car track north of Twin Falls. No data on Idaho roadster purses is available but most were probably less than $250. The payoff for a main event win was, at most, about $40.

This may be a fatal blow to some flathead V8 lovers but the dominant car in Idaho roadster racing was, of all things, a NASH! The car was owned and built by the shop foreman at a Twin Falls Nash dealership. The power plant was a modified Ambassador Six and the dealership was the sponsor. Lloyd Libert was the driver and he probably won more Idaho roadster races than anybody. Libert remembers that, "The Nash Ambassador Six was an excellent engine with good torque for the loose dirt tracks that we ran". Like most Idaho track roadsters Libert's Nash was built for track racing and was not a converted street rod.

Besides Lloyd Libert, some of the other Idaho roadster drivers who did well were Paul Whaley, Leon Evans, Bill Bishoff and Denny Dike. Despite the dangers of running on the horse tracks there were no serious injuries in the Idaho racing.

A couple of questions on Idaho roadster racing remain. Where did the "roadsters" that raced at Moscow around 1930 come from? (See *Roaring Roadsters*). It is strange that there was no roadster racing in Idaho's biggest city, Boise. If there was any kind of a roadster group there it has been completely forgotten. The SIRA was headquartered a couple of hundred miles to the east and never made it to Boise.

Lloyd Libert slides inside of a competitor during a race on an Idaho horse track.

All photos from the Lloyd Libert Collection.

Lloyd Libert in his first roadster ride. Although most Idaho cars were built for the track this one appears to be a converted street rod

An unidentified driver at an unidentified Idaho track. The engine appears stock but with the lightweight chassis it should have been a fairly fast car.

Action at a night race. This is probably at the stock car track north of Twin Falls in about 1954.

A car gets sideways and kicks up a lot of dust and dirt. The volcanic soil of southeastern Idaho was very abrasive and the dust "ate up engines."

Downtown Twin Falls with Lloyd Libert at the wheel of the very neat Nash Ambassador Six. The chassis and most other parts are Nash. Can anybody identify the body?

Illinois

Roadster racing in Illinois began in 1931 when a series of "Stock Car" races were held at various cities. Most of the information on this racing comes from Indy vet Emil Andres who still prefers to refer to the roadsters as stock cars. In most of the races, Andres drove a stripped Model A roadster with a Miller Schofield overhead valve engine. There was no actual roadster group formed and very few rules other than that closed cars were not allowed. Most of the races were on a mile horse track at Evanston, but there were also races at Aurora and on tracks in Indiana and Wisconsin. The drivers included some big names other than Emil Andres—Indy drivers Duke Nalon and Paul Russo as well as midget great Cowboy O'Rourke. Andres remembers that most of the purses were small and under $500 but he had a good day at Evanston and took home $94. In 1931 dollars that was better than most roadster racers did in a career.

Most, if not all, of the other prewar roadster rac-

Emil Andres in his 1931 "Stock Car." The Model A engine had a Miller-Schofield OHV engine. Andres became a star in the midgets and big cars and competed at Indianapolis 12 times. (Andres Collection)

Evanston in 1932. Emil Andres is on the pole in #77 with Cowboy O'Rourke on the outside. Duke Nalon and Paul Russo may also be in the photo. (Jim Haag Collection-Bob Sheldon Photo)

Another view of the Evanston track in about 1932. Although the one-mile oval was called Evanston Speedway, it was basically a horse track. (Jim Haag Collection-Bob Sheldon Photo)

ing in Illinois was closer to jalopy racing. For the most part the cars were called "Hobos." This racing was on county fair ovals as well as on off-road courses. The rules, if any, were liberal and some cars had modified engines. Hobo races were held at Quincy, Hull, Jacksonville, Tuscola and Aledo.

In postwar roadster racing Andy Granatelli's Hurricane Racing Association got most of the publicity. Hurricane sanctioned races at Chicago's Soldier field and drew huge crowds. Attendance figures vary from those reported in NSSN, those advertised by Hurricane and those remembered by racers. These numbers vary from 21,000 to 60,000 but are no doubt the largest crowds ever to see the hot rods race. Hurricane also held races at Springfield, Rockford and several other Illinois cities. The Hurricane roadsters didn't last very long as the stock cars took over and were far better suited to Andy Granatelli's remarkable promotional talents. Among Hurricane's top drivers were Willy Sternquist, Ray Erickson and Al Swenson. Visitors, attracted by the big purses at Soldier Field, included Dick Frazier (who took home a lot of money), Jim and Dick Rathmann, Pat Flaherty and Don Freeland.

Another Illinois roadster group was the Tri-State Hot Rod Racing Association which called Prather

A strange mixture of cars lines up for an "Old Car Race" at Jacksonville in 1938. Only a few are even close to being track roadsters. (Leslie Ankrom Collection)

This car, whatever it is called, is a Buick and it won the race at Jacksonville in 1938. (Leslie Ankrom Collection)

Speedway in De Kalb its' home track. Under the able leadership of George Stafford this group ran regularly at Prather and had occasional races at Streator, Waukegan and in Wausau, Indiana. The Tri State racers ran for purses that seldom exceeded $500 as Stan Scheidecker and Bill Seaman won most of the races.

It is possible that there were other roadster groups in Illinois. This includes a Tri-States Auto Racing Alliance, a midget organization, which planned to sanction roadster races in the southern part of Illinois and in adjoining Indiana and Kentucky.

Rolling Roadsters is a group that was almost lost to roadster history. They raced but one year and only at four tracks in Illinois and Indiana. Just recently, Don Anderson of Dayton, Ohio stumbled upon Rolling Roadsters in some 1948 issues of *Illustrated Speedway News.*

Al Swenson was listed as the 1948 champion of Rolling Roadsters. Anderson called Swenson, a longtime friend, and the history of the group came to light.

Rolling Roadsters was organized in early 1948 by Chicago speed shop owner Bill Von Esser. There were a number of nearby tracks that wanted to run the roadsters but Andy Granatelli's Hurricane Racing Association was too busy to provide dates. Von Esser's roadsters filled the void and Rolling Roadsters ran 15 dates at Crown Point and South Bend in Indiana and Danville and Mendota, Illinois. Although the group had car count problems at some tracks, the crowds were big and the payoffs (an average of $1200) were excellent. For no visible reason, Rolling Roadsters lasted only one year. The drivers who ran with the group include: Al Swenson, Bill Von Esser, Herman Jordan, Willy Sternquist, Lyman Lee, Bud Stone, Nick Carrzone and Jim Boore.

OK—so what? Check the La Salle entry list—half a dozen are known Rolling Wheels drivers. Check the logo on the program cover—car #V-1 is Bill Von Esser's V8. So—the mysterious La Salle (non-) racers were Rolling Roadsters members. It is still not known why they didn't race that night, why the Hurricane hotshots showed up and why Rolling Roadsters wasn't mentioned on the program.

EVENT NO. 1—TIME TRIALS—ENTRIES

Driver's Name	No.	Make	Time
Alfred Konger	A.K.O.	V-8 Spl.	
Herman Jordan	Mar-El Spl.	V-8	
John Pericles	33	V-8	
Jack Hubert	19	V-8	
Howard Bochte	32	Chev.	
Bill Von Esser (Bud Stone)	V-1	V-8	19.82 12
Moose Carlson	12	V-8	
Fritz Monroe	Mar-El Spl. 7	V-8	
Crash Clark		V-8	
Bob Schermerhorn		Crager	
Lyman Lee	13	Chev.	
Buddy Taylor		Plymouth	
Joel Watamade	Dee Spl.	Chev.	
Kenny Kottlie	Miller-Schofield	Model A	
Charles Foxworthy		Chev.	
Myrle Dickey	2X	V-8	
Bud Stone	8	V-8	
Ray Smith		V-8	
Joe Liebich	23	V-8	
Henry Geiser	32	V-8	
Gene Marmor	6	V-8	
Kenney Netzel	38	V-8	
Nick Carrzone	22	V-8	
Jim Boore	4½	Model A	
Added Entries—			
[illegible]	111		18.55 8
[illegible]	64		18.56 9
[illegible]	42		18.53 6
[illegible]	8		17.30 4
[illegible]	0		18.76 10
[illegible]	38		19.84 12
Jim Bothman	16		16.01 2
[illegible]	9		16.51 3
[illegible]	7		18.80 11
Art Davis	71		18.31 7
[illegible]	104		20.02 14
[illegible]	01		15.98 1

There are not many familiar names printed on this entry list but most, or all, are members of the nearly lost Rolling Roadsters group. (Bob Fanning Collection)

This program is for "Hot Rod Auto Races" but, unfortunately, there is no mention of a sanctioning body. (Bob Fanning Collection)

A SOLDIER FIELD MYSTERY

You may wonder why there are so few Soldier Field roadster photos in this book. So, do I. There must have been hundreds of photos taken there. Bob Sheldon is the premier photographer-collector in that part of the country—he has found a grand total of ten Soldier Field hot rod photos. Bruce Craig has tens of thousands of racing photos from all over the country—his Soldier Field roadster collection is zero. Over the years, photos taken by other photographers have found their way into the collections of people like Sheldon and Craig. These should have included Soldier Field roadsters.

Some 5000 roadster photos have found their way to Idaho and my collection. None of the thousands of photos were from Soldier Field. Where are all the Soldier Field roadster photos?

Al Swenson bounces off a hay bale and heads for the photographer at Soldier Field. Swenson was one of the regulars with Andy Granatelli's Hurricane Racing Association. (Bob Sheldon Photo)

An unidentified driver smacks the wall at Soldier Field. Spectator protection is minimal. (Bob Sheldon Photo)

This Jacksonville car is stripped to near nothing. Looks like there were not many rules. (Leslie Ankrom Collection)

On the way to the races at De Kalb in 1950. Only the rich "teams" had trailers. (Dick Schultz Collection)

De Kalb in 1949. The driver of this V8 is Nels Edam. (Bob Fanning Collection)

Action at Prather Speedway in De Kalb. Dick Schultz is in #34 but the other drivers cannot be identified. (Dick Schultz Collection)

Dick Schultz raced a channeled '34 roadster with a mildly hopped up V8. While not a big winner, he was competitive at De Kalb and other tracks. (Richard Adams Photo—Dick Schultz Collection)

Car #51 is probably Bill Seaman's ride. Seaman won a lot of De Kalb races before being killed at that track. (Bob Fanning Collection)

This photo was probably taken at De Kalb in 1949. That is a very unusual magneto—perhaps an aircraft adaptation? (Dick Schultz Collection)

The Stan Scheidecker Merc used a narrowed Model A body. A nice looking car and a winner. (Bob Fanning Collection)

HOWARD LINNE

Any fan who has seen a USAC midget race in the last 45 years has probably seen one of Howard Linne's cars compete. Linne has fielded top-flight midgets in USAC events all over the country. His drivers have included names like Troy Ruttman, A.J. Foyt, Parnelli Jones and Johnny Rutherford. His cars have won 69 USAC main events and, with Jimmy Davies, the 1961 National Midget Championship.

Howard Linne started racing in 1940 in equipment that was a bit less sophisticated than the three midgets he is still fielding. Linne ran in a jalopy circuit in and around the town of Henry in northern Illinois. The cars were jalopies in name only—actually, they were big cars or roadsters without bodies. Safety was ignored. There was a rollbar of sorts but no seat belt, no helmet and not even a firewall! Engine modifications were allowed and Linne's car had what was close to a typical big car engine of that era. It was a 1928 four-cylinder Chevy with an Oldsmobile three-port head and other hop up goodies. This usually included (longer) Durant rods to increase the compression. Linne must have been on a limited budget—he simply welded a one-inch extension in the stock Chevy rods!

As with the midgets later on, Linne was a winner in these primitive machines. He won a number of main events and was, as reported in the October 16, 1941 issue of *National Auto Racing News*, a contender in the "Illinois State Jallopy (sic) Championship" race. While battling for the lead in a preliminary event Linne flipped his jalopy and suffered a broken collarbone.

After World War II Linne drove a few midgets races but found he preferred the role of car owner. Howard Linne was recently inducted into the USAC Midget Hall of Fame. A well deserved honor.

In 1941, Howard Linne drove this car in Illinois jalopy races. That is a full race 1928 Chevy four-cylinder engine. The car was faster than many of the big cars and roadsters of that time. Shown with Howard Linne is his brother, Herb, who helped build the car. (Linne Collection)

A dazed Howard Linne is on his way to the hospital after a 1941 crash at Henry. He has a broken collarbone. (Linne Collection)

The jalopies line up for the start at Henry in 1940. On the pole is Howard Linne in a very stripped down Model A Ford. (Linne Collection—Gray Photo)

The late 1970s and times have changed—the Howard Linne Offy midget at Phoenix. Left to right is driver Lee Kunzman, Linne and car builder Don Edmunds. (Linne Collection)

Stan Scheidecker hit something very solid at De Kalb. Note the lack of an idler on the water pump belt—a common track practice. (Dick Schultz Collection)

Either R. Case or Glenn Taylor drove this neat looking Tri-States Hot Rod Association Merc. (Bob Fanning Collection)

Stan Scheidecker looks relaxed as he waits to race at De Kalb. Had the Tri-States group bothered to crown a champion it would have been Scheidecker. (Bob Fanning Collection)

The cars line up for the feature event at De Kalb. No identification on any of the drivers. (Ivan Prall Collection)

This is Chuck Wolfe of Chicago. Reportedly, this was a "California car" but, often, any nice looking car would be advertised as such. (Bob Fanning Collection)

De Kalb in 1949. Left to right are car builder Rolla Covert, driver Stan Scheidecker, sponsor "Chris" and Bob Fanning. Check that steering gear! (Bob Fanning Collection)

Earl Walker is shown with his V8. The use of stock heads was not uncommon on Illinois roadsters. (Bob Fanning Collection)

Dick Schultz in #34 leads the pack at De Kalb. That fence looks a bit unsafe. (Dick Schultz Collection)

THE QUINCY RACERS

Lee Davis tells a marvelous story of racing at Quincy in the late 1930s. The racing started out at Baldwin Park with stripped strictly stock cars manufactured before 1926. Billed as "The Tin Can Derby" there were some dusty races at Quincy and on horse tracks in Illinois and Missouri.

Like all racers, the drivers wanted to go faster and the rules kept changing. Soon 1928 models were allowed, as were engine modifications, and the cars became a lot closer to track roadsters. Some very interesting cars were raced at Baldwin Park and nearby tracks. Bud Hack built a Stutz with a huge eight-cylinder motor. John Joy had a '28 Chevy with a four-cylinder Plymouth engine with a Graham Paige Supercharger. There were also the more conventional hopped up Model As and Chevies with the Olds three-port head. Most of the cars sound as though they were quite fast. A probable exception was the car of Russ Gross who had a cutdown Meteor Hearst with a six-cylinder Plymouth engine.

Lee Davis helped his friend Leigh Miller build a modified four-cylinder Nash. This was a beautiful engine with overhead valves but the lower end was very weak with only two main bearings. Davis and Miller tried to drive the car to the racetrack only to have a rod go out after four blocks. It was back to the drawing board and shop to install a six-cylinder Nash. This was a fast machine but, sadly, Leigh Miller was killed in the car at Middletown, Missouri.

It is unfortunate that no photos of the unusual Quincy cars are known to exist.

SOMETHING STRANGE AT LA SALLE

A roadster race was held on Friday night July 16, 1948 at La Salle some 50 miles west of Chicago. The printed program lists the names of 24 cars and drivers. Only Herman Jordan is a familiar name. With one exception, none of these cars and drivers competed that night. There were 12 write-ins on the program. De Kalb driver Stan Scheidecker was entered as well as Hurricane hot shots Jim Rathmann, Al Swenson and Ray Erickson. Since these drivers were entered, it was probably a Hurricane promotion. Swenson, Rathmann and Erickson outqualified the field by three to five seconds and ran one, two, three in the main event.

Who were the drivers who did not race that night? Were they boycotting the event or simply not invited? Were they members of a La Salle roadster group that has been forgotten?

Note: The above sidebar appears to be an Illinois roadster racing mystery that will never be solved. The sidebar on page 56 was written some six months later and, at first, seems totally unrelated to La Salle.

A De Kalb crash in 1949. Looks like the V8 engine is laying on the ground. (Bob Fanning Collection)

Marvin Prather promoted successful roadster races at De Kalb for two seasons. (Bob Fanning Collection)

This is Waukegan in 1949. Dick Schultz is in the Scheidecker Merc and he won the main event. (Dick Schultz Collection)

A photo of Pat Flaherty was used on the program cover for this 1951 Chicago Hot Rod Show. By then, Flaherty was an established Indy driver. (Jim Fortin Collection)

Indiana

With the exception of California, Indiana had more roadster racing than any other state. The cars were good, the drivers were good and the purses were good.

The first roadster racing in Indiana was in the early 1930s when the loosely organized group based in Evanston, Illinois ventured into Indiana for some races. Roadster races were held in Crown Point, Wolf Lake and on the high banks of Winchester. It is almost certain that there was some sort of roadster group in Indiana during this period but nothing has surfaced.

Roadster racing really got going in Indiana in late 1938 when the Mutual Stock Car Racing Association formed. The first Mutual sanctioned races were on an off-road "steeplechase" course at Muncie in 1939. In 1940 Mutual took to the oval tracks and, primarily under the leadership of Dutch Hurst, began to build a strong base of cars, drivers and tracks. When racing was halted by World War II in August of 1942 Mutual was racing regularly at tracks like Mt Lawn, Winchester and Fort Wayne. There is little doubt that Mutual's purses were the best in the country with guarantees of $500.

With a strong organization in place, Mutual was the first roadster group to race after WW II. Races were held in 1945 only a few weeks after the government ban on racing was lifted and Dick Frazier was crowned the champion for that year. In 1947 Mutual voted to remove the words "stock car" from their name and became the Mutual Racing Association (MRA). This group would dominate Indiana roadster racing. Mutual considered Mt Lawn (a track that still exists today) it's home track but held frequent races at tracks like Winchester, Fort Wayne, South Bend, Kokomo, Salem, Sun Valley and at Dayton and the Cincinnati Speedbowl in Ohio.

Strangely enough, it took the MRA car owners awhile to discover the Ford and Mercury V8 engines that were winning races in other parts of the country. The thinking in Mutual was that a long stroke engine like the Hudson or Ford Six was the best bet. This thinking was changed in 1948 when Dick Frazier and Hack Winninger fielded the famous #32 roadster with a West Coast built Merc V8.

Thanks To Joe Helpling, the MRA helped found a race that has become one of today's biggest sprint car races. This is the "Little 500" at Anderson. Helpling scheduled the first 500-lap race on this steeply banked quarter mile oval in 1949. The Mutual car owners and drivers thought he was nuts and pleaded for a shorter race. They were convinced that none of their roadsters would last that long. Helpling was adamant that 500 laps would be the distance, "even if we have to come back the next day for somebody to finish". He was also right and the MRA put on a fine show as Sam Skinner won the race. MRA roadsters ran this race until 1955 when the sprints took over. The 1950 "Little 500" paid $9578 and was almost certainly the largest ever roadster payoff.

Action at the Muncie Steeplechase track in 1939. This racer has some 1990s "down tubes" reinforcing his Chevy. (Remington-Hurst Collection)

A field of early Mutual roadsters battle in the dust at Muncie. (Remington-Hurst Collection)

There was other roadster groups that raced in Indiana. Andy Granatelli's Hurricane Racing Association ran some races at 16th Street Speedway in Indianapolis. There was a "Midwest Hot Rod Association," the "Southern Indiana Racing Association" and the "Universal Racing Association." Almost certainly, there were dozens of unsanctioned and forgotten roadster races in Indiana.

The top Indiana roadster drivers include Dick Frazier, Tom Cherry, Smokey Stover, George Tichenor, Wayne Alspaugh, Red Renner, Curly Boyd, Everette Burton, Larry Crockett, Dale Swaim, Billy Earl and Pat O'Connor. Visitors who did OK include Roy Prosser, Jim Rathmann, Red Amick and Jim Rigsby.

Thanks to Dale Fairfax of Indianapolis for an exceptional amount of help with this chapter.

The Joe Walls car, probably at Muncie, in 1939. Walls was one of the better Mutual car builders and even in this early photo headers and the frame mounted radius rods are evident. (Joe Walls Collection)

Lined up for the start at Muncie in 1939. Removing the door was one way to get elbowroom for the driver. With no seat belt, this did not exactly enhance driver safety. (Remington-Hurst Collection)

Sam Skinner at Mt Lawn Speedway in 1940. It looks like helmets were not required. (Don Anderson Collection)

This is Mt Lawn Speedway in 1941. The Mutual roadsters get ready for a race on the odd shaped track. (Don Anderson Collection)

WINCHESTER

Few tracks are as rich in history and tradition as Winchester. Few are as deadly. Frank Funk built the track in 1914. At that time the track was flat and was simply known as Funk's Speedway. Over the years the track acquired it's famed high banks and became known as Winchester Speedway.

It is believed that the unnamed Illinois roadster group raced at Winchester in the early 1930s but there is no specific information on these races. It can be documented that the roadsters ran at Winchester on September 10, 1939. Frank Funk advertised "Hopped-up Stock Car Races" as an additional attraction at four Central States Racing Association big car races that fall. It would seem likely that the nearby Mutual Stock Car Association would supply the cars but in 1939, this group was still running steeplechase events at Muncie. Maybe some Mutual cars were running oval races that late in the season or the cars came from an unknown roadster group.

Mutual did run races at Winchester from 1940 until 1942 and then again in the postwar roadster era. The track in those years was much as it is today—paved and with about the same degree of banking. It was not nearly as smooth and did not have the concrete crash wall. For most of the time the roadsters raced there, the crash wall was made of two-inch steel pipe. There are records of this pipe impaling cars but, fortunately, no drivers. In retrospect, it was a terrible place to race with the mostly ill handling cars and rookie drivers.

Nonetheless, somebody said, "race," so Mutual raced and raced fast. Speeds were close to the top sprint cars of the day. On June 20, 1948 Dick Frazier made headlines by breaking Ted Horn's Offy track record at Winchester. Driving the Hack Winninger #32 Mercury the talented Frazier turned a lap of 21.37 seconds. That calculates to 84.2 mph. A bit down from today's speeds but hey, you modern guys, try it with one quarter the tire surface and horsepower!

Mutual raced at Winchester until about 1952 and Frazier's record was broken in the later years. The racing was not without a price. Mutual driver, Freddie Wingate died there in a 1946 crash.

'Grand Old Man of the Nation's Auto Racing

FRANK FUNK'S
SPEEDWAY ENTERPRISES
SPEEDWAY CAR SCHEDULE
Class "A" and "B" Events

Completing 24 Years at the World's Fastest Bowl!
WINCHESTER. INDIANA
8—EVENTS—8 SEASON'S FINAL
SUNDAY, SEPTEMBER 10—PURSE $1,600

World's Highest Banked Bowl
FT. WAYNE (Ind.) SPEEDWAY
8—EVENTS—8 SPRINT RACES
SUNDAY, SEPTEMBER 17—PURSE, $1,600

JUNGLE PARK—ROCKVILLE, IND.—CLASS "A" AND "B"
SUNDAY, OCTOBER 1—PURSE $1,500

DAYTON, OHIO—8—EVENTS—8 CLASS "A" AND "B"
SUNDAY, OCTOBER 8—PURSE $1,600

PLUS HOPPED-UP STOCK CAR RACES

For Information on Frank Funk Races, Write
FUNK'S SPEEDWAY ENTERPRISES, Winchester, Ind.

This ad appeared in the August 31, 1939 issue of National Auto Racing News. The "Hopped-up Stock Cars" are most likely the first national mention of the roadsters. (Dale Fairfax Collection)

The Mutual roadsters line up for a 1947 race on a rough Winchester Speedway. That scary looking crash wall is made out of two-inch pipe. (Zane Howell Collection)

Jim Morrison leaves Winchester in a cloud of dust. Morrison virtually destroyed the Strabler #39 but escaped with minor injuries. (Jack Hathaway Collection)

Dick Frazier smiles after breaking Ted Horn's AAA sprint car record at Winchester. (Bill Hill Collection)

The Dick Frazier-Hack Winninger Mercury is shown in the Transportation exhibit at the Smithsonian Museum in Washington DC. An honor for both roadster racing and Don Anderson who restored #32. (Don Anderson Collection)

Floyd Robbins gets ready for a race at Mt. Lawn. He was one of the better prewar drivers. (George Tichenor Collection)

Smokey Stover is shown in the Joe Walls Hudson powered Model A after a win at Mt. Lawn in 1940. (Joe Walls Collection)

This program cover is from 1947 and Mutual is still calling the roadsters "Stock Cars" (Zane Howell Collection)

Mutual roadsters line up for a race at Mt. Lawn. That should be Dick Frazier in the "Greyhound" bringing up the rear. (George Tichenor Collection)

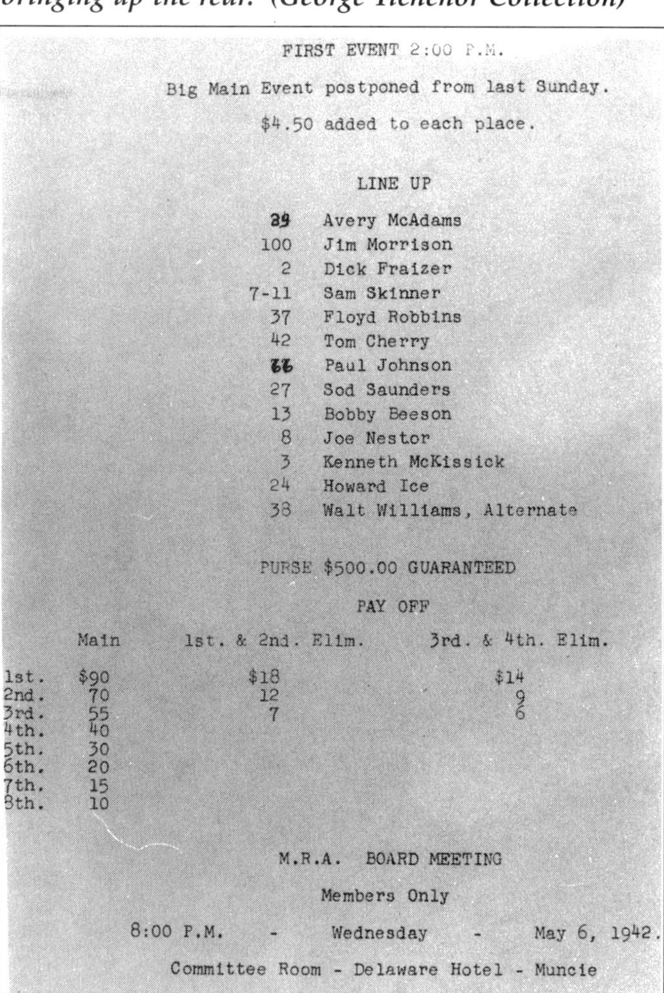

FIRST EVENT 2:00 P.M.

Big Main Event postponed from last Sunday.

$4.50 added to each place.

LINE UP

39 Avery McAdams
100 Jim Morrison
2 Dick Fraizer
7-11 Sam Skinner
37 Floyd Robbins
42 Tom Cherry
66 Paul Johnson
27 Sod Saunders
13 Bobby Beeson
8 Joe Nestor
3 Kenneth McKissick
24 Howard Ice
38 Walt Williams, Alternate

PURSE $500.00 GUARANTEED

PAY OFF

	Main	1st. & 2nd. Elim.	3rd. & 4th. Elim.
1st.	$90	$18	$14
2nd.	70	12	9
3rd.	55	7	6
4th.	40		
5th.	30		
6th.	20		
7th.	15		
8th.	10		

M.R.A. BOARD MEETING

Members Only

8:00 P.M. - Wednesday - May 6, 1942.

Committee Room - Delaware Hotel - Muncie

This notice was mailed out to Mutual members after a May 1942 rainout at Mt. Lawn. (Don Anderson Collection)

Wild action at Mt. Lawn in about 1940. Look at that crowd! (Remington-Hurst Collection)

Howard Ice in about 1946. Not too many Mutual cars used the '27 Model T bodies but Ice was one of them. (Joe Walls Collection)

A fine view of the Mt. Lawn track in 1946. Smokey Stover is on the pole in the Joe Walls Terraplane with Dick Frazier on the outside in the Cox Model A. (Joe Walls Collection)

Mt. Lawn in 1946. The spectators had a close up view of the action but with minimal protection from the cars. (Joe Walls Collection)

Sam Skinner is in the Meterpaugh Chevy at Mt. Lawn. This is 1946 or 1947. (Meterpaugh Collection)

Dick Frazier at Winchester in 1946 or 1947. Frazier took a trip over the wall in the background in this car. (Dick Frazier Collection)

Dan Walls is shown with driver Freddie Wingate at Mt. Lawn. Wingate lost his life in a Winchester roadster crash. (Tichenor Collection)

Left–There was no fancy hauler for George Tichenor's roadster at Mt. Lawn. Just dump everything in the racecar and tow it home. (George Tichenor Collection)

TOM CHERRY

The Tom Cherry roadster is shown at an Indiana track in 1949. The attention to details like the rear bumper (nerfing iron) was unusual. (Dale Fairfax Collection)

The front bumper of #38 got the same treatment. The bodywork is exceptional. (Don Anderson Collection)

Even the trailer displayed exceptional attention to detail and neatness. Few racers bothered with this type of workmanship—a trailer was lucky to get painted. (Tom Cherry Jr. Collection)

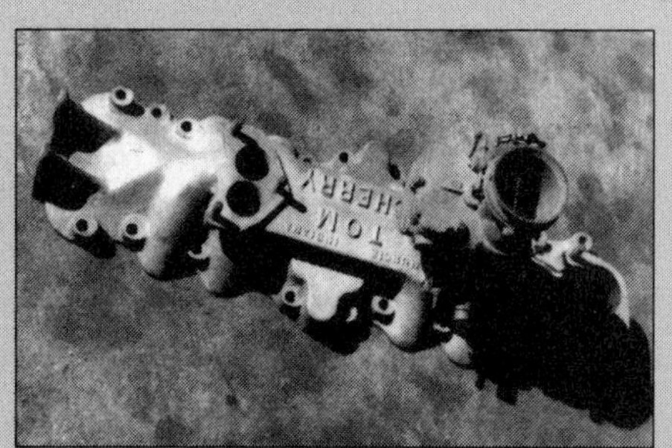

Cherry cast his own intake manifolds for Ford or Mercury V8s. He sold a lot of them. (Mike Quick Collection)

The Tom Cherry Mercury today. Don Anderson of Dayton, Ohio has restored it to NASCAR specifications. Anderson re-introduced #38 to the high banks of Winchester in 1996. (Don Anderson Photo)

Tom Cherry is pictured in his beautiful sprint car. This is the roadster chassis. The photo was taken in front of Cherry's Muncie speed shop. (Remington-Hurst Collection)

Tom Cherry excelled as a driver, car builder, speed shop operator and race promoter. He was an important part of the roadster scene in Indiana.

Cherry's name is associated with the Mutual Racing Association from the beginning. He may or may not have participated in the Muncie Steeplechase races but when Mutual took to the ovals Tom Cherry was there. He was the 1940 Mutual champion and in the late 1940s won more than his share of races. Cherry won the Little 500 at Anderson four times. Cherry was also a winner in the midgets and in the sprints.

Tom Cherry operated a speed shop in Muncie and supplied area racers with parts. He was noted for giving a car owner a break by advancing credit but was also noted for hanging around the race-track payoff window and collecting debts. He was a good businessman.

In about 1949 Tom Cherry started driving the Hack Winnegar-Basil Bense built #38 roadster. It appears that Cherry "produced" the machine like a modern Penske. The car was one of the best looking in Indiana and it ran fast and consistently. As the roadsters started to die out Cherry purchased the car and helped convert #38 into a beautiful sprint car. Later on, the Mercury powered machine was stretched to a 96-inch wheelbase and successfully raced in NASCAR's short lived Speedway Division.

In the mid-1950s, Cherry was the driving force behind the All American Racing Club. This group ran sprint car races in Indiana, Michigan and Ohio.

Avery McAdams pulls into the pits at Mt. Lawn in 1946. McAdams is driving the Walt Stabler Ford Six. (Joe Walls Collection)

Sprint car driver Billy Earl was a regular with the Southern Indiana Racing Association. Here he gets a trophy at Franklin. (Billy Earl Collection)

DISSENSION

It seems that there is an unwritten rule in racing that if things are going really well, something will happen to cause problems. It is as if the racers have a meeting and decide, "Hey, things look great. What can we do to louse it up?" Usually the "solution" is to form another racing group to split the cars, drivers and the crowds. Fortunately, this sort of thing does not happen anymore. Observe how stable the Indy Car racing scene is these days. Maybe all those rich people are smarter than we hot rod racers were?

The splitting of a successful roadster racing program into two less than successful groups was common in the roadster era. It happened in California. It happened in Indiana.

The Mutual Racing Association had a very good year in 1947 and things looked even better for 1948. The problem began at the annual election of officers. Roger Cox, who owned the 1947 Championship car, decided that his close personal friend, Ray Huddleson, should be elected president. No doubt, Cox meant well but when the election went against them, Cox and Huddleson stormed out of the meeting in anger. Cox soon founded another roadster group, Universal Racing Association, and apparently set out to destroy Mutual.

Cox had his 1947 champion driver, Avery McAdams, on his side and managed to convince other Mutual people to come along with Universal. Cox scheduled races at the New Castle Fairgrounds only a few miles from Mutual's most successful track, Mt . Lawn Speedway.

Details are sparse but Mutual was a tough competitor. Universal tried some races at Richmond and Greensburg but ran into dust problems at both tracks. It is probable that Lloyd Stanbrook was killed at Greensburg in a Universal race. The next week at Greensburg the dust was so bad the race was canceled. So far as anybody can remember that was the end of the Universal Racing Association.

See the Hot Rod Boys Pile Into Those Wide Turns 3 Abreast

EVERY SATURDAY NIGHT AT

NEW CASTLE'S FAIRGROUNDS TRACK

11 Cars Competed Last Week for a Crowd That Was Completely Satisfied.

EVERY SATURDAY NIGHT

SPEED ... SPEED ... THRILLS

SENSATIONAL! WE'VE GOT IT!

The Answer to a Race Fans Dream—

INVERTED MAIN EVENT!

Nothing Like It in Indiana Before!

ROARING ROADSTER

RACES

SUNDAY NIGHT—8:30

MT. LAWN

SPEEDWAY

★ MUTUAL RACING ASSOCIATION ★

The Old Reliable!

Popular Prices 85¢ bleachers

Universal Racing Association ran the upper ad in the Muncie newspaper. Their attempt to compete with "The Old Reliable" Mutual Racing Association was not successful. (Jon Gullihier Collection)

Future Indy winner Pat Flaherty visited the Mutual Racing Association in 1948. There is no record of how he fared in the California Roadster Association car. (Steve Quirk Collection)

Dan Walls built this Merc for the Southern Indiana Racing Association. The car has a wide sprint type body. (Dan Walls Collection)

Future Indy winner Jim Rathmann winds up as "Jim Rathmore" in this 1949 Winchester photo. Note how little protection he has in this car. (Bud Williams photo from Midwest Auto Racing Annual—1950)

The unusual shape of Mt Lawn Speedway is evident in this aerial photo. The terrain dictated the shape. (Meterpaugh Collection)

Howard Mowell has an embarrassing moment in the Lee Izor Chevy. This must have been before safety hubs were required. (Izor Collection)

Dale Swain is in the Don Hobson Ford at Mellott. Swain was a regular in the Midwest Hot Rod Association. (Swain Collection)

Winchester on October 14, 1949 and Wayne Alspaugh has just won the feature in the Robinson Merc. Can we assume that an auto body shop was NOT a sponsor? (Wayne Alspaugh Collection)

Jim McWithey gets a trophy from Mutual Racing Association boss Dutch Hurst. Mt. Lawn in 1952. (Remington-Hurst Collection)

Winchester in 1949. Announcer Dutch Hurst is shown with (left to right) Larry Crockett, Roy Prosser and Jim Morrison. (Remington-Hurst Collection)

Here We Go Again!

Roaring Roadster

Auto Races

SUNDAY NIGHT

8:30 P. M.

MT. LAWN

★ **SPEEDWAY** ★

— West of New Castle —

The Speedway has been completely renovated and sprayed — The food will be inspected.

All precautions for sanitation and cleanliness wil be taken.

The effects of a polio scare are reflected in this Mutual ad. Racing was stopped for several weeks because of the epidemic. (Dick Frazier Collection)

Everette Burton is shown with the ex-Dick Frazier-Hack Winninger Merc. Burton won his share of races in this very fast car. (Dale Fairfax Collection)

The Columbus (Indiana) Fairgrounds in 1948 and one of the few Mutual races on dirt. Junior Fort usually drove this Sherm Van Dyke Ford Six. (Izor Collection)

The Mutual roadsters get ready to race at Winchester. Number 66 is the Bennett Brothers car. (Dale Fairfax Collection)

Western star Roy Rogers served as Grand Marshall of the 1954 Little 500. Joe Helpling always did a good job of promoting at Anderson (aka Sun Valley Speedway) (Bob Hoover Collection)

This should be the Bob Doyscher DeSoto V8 from Minnesota. Rick Kerr is probably the driver at the 1954 Little 500. (Remington Collection)

Jack Goodwin of Detroit drove the Edgar Beste Merc in the 1953 Little 500 at Anderson. He finished 12th. (Remington-Hurst Collection)

Smokey Stover in the Joe Walls Hudson. This was in 1950 and, although the V8s were starting to dominate, the Joe Walls car was still more than competitive. (Joe Walls Collection)

Leon Waltz is shown with the Lowell Waltz V8 powered T at Mt. Iowa in 1941. Watz was killed in this car a few weeks after. (Dan Walls Collection)

The first Donald Hobson roadster at Jungle Park in about 1948. The car has a license—perhaps it was driven to the track? (Hobson Collection)

Bill Russell of Danville IL at Jungle Park. For some reason, most Jungle Park cars were crude. (Hobson Collection)

Not a clear photo—not a beautiful car. Jungle Park in about 1950. (Hobson Collection)

Iowa

Iowa has always been a hotbed of auto racing and there was plenty of roadster racing in the state. Surprisingly, very little has shown up on prewar Iowa roadster racing. Certainly, this is because it has not been found rather than it did not exist. It is possible that there was a South Dakota-Iowa roadster circuit in the early 1930s.

Driver Butch Baker and rider, Alva McCoy get ready for a 1940 race at Corning. Winning the 50 lapper paid all of $16. (Alva McCoy Collection)

The only definite evidence of roadster racing comes from the adventures of Alva McCoy at the Adams County Fairgrounds in Corning in 1940. The race was probably billed as a stock car or jalopy event but from the variety of the field, it was definitely "run what you brung." In the ten car starting field was a Buick, a Whippet, some assorted Fords and a 1928 Stutz Bearcat coupe. This car, owned by the Bragg Motor Company in Corning, was definitely the high dollar entry. Bragg Motors paid $100 for it. Joining the field was Butch Barker and Alva McCoy from nearby Gravity, Iowa. McCoy had stripped his Model A Ford roadster to near nothing so it had a huge weight advantage over the field. Butch Barker was to be the driver and McCoy had no intention of competing. Somewhat to his horror, he found that a riding mechanic was required so he went along for what turned out to be a wild ride.

The Barker-McCoy team outran and outlasted the field and came home a winner over the Stutz. The payoff was all of $16. Barker later raced other cars but for Alva McCoy that was it. He explains, "I'd stripped the Model A to the point where there was nothing for me to hang on to—that race was enough for me!"

After World War II roadster racing in Iowa did not get started until 1949. Prior to that, there had been some form of jalopy racing and the roadsters were, at least partially, an evolution of these cars. There were at least five roadster associations formed in Iowa. The strongest groups were the Central Iowa Racing Association (CIRA) and the Hawkeye Hot Rod Association (HHRA) The two groups apparently cooperated with each other and some cars and drivers ran with both organizations.

The CIRA ran mostly on county fair tracks in the central part of the state. Quite often, there would be two-day meets in conjunction with county fairs. Some of the top drivers were Jimmy Maddox, Kenny Cook, Nate Grassfield and Speed Lyman.

The Hawkeye Hot Rod Association also ran some county fair tracks but they had pretty much of a "home" track with regular races at Pioneer (aka Kessell) Speedway in Des Moines. There were also quite a few races at Marshalltown where, more or less, the same group of drivers ran under the sanction of the Central Iowa Hot Rod Association. There is no record of the CIHRA having crowned a champion but, had they bothered, it would probably have been Kenny Higginson. Higginson is listed as the winner of many races at Pioneer Speedway and at Marshalltown. Other top drivers were Lue Holland and Bobby VanHossen.

Most of the data available on Iowa roadster racing is from 1950 to 1954. The last known roadster race was at Pioneer Speedway in 1956. This was a combined show with the sprint cars and a poster for the event advertised "Truck Roadster and Splint Car Race." Looks like the promoter needed to do a bit of proofreading!

Warren Brooklander is pictured someplace in Iowa. That's a motorcycle tire on the left front—a common track practice. (Len Lloyd Collection)

Billy Richardson is in the Buss Shade Shop Merc. This is probably at Pioneer (aka Kessell) Speedway in Des Moines. (Len Lloyd Collection)

Cecil Maddox was one of the top Iowa roadster drivers. He is shown in the Phil Ponds Merc in 1949. (Len Lloyd Collection)

Bob Snyder owned this roadster and George Seifert (left) drove it. It is not known where the pair competed. (Bob Snyder Collection)

Mahoney's Farm near Davenport in 1949. It was supposed to be a roadster race but not enough cars showed up so the promoter let the spectators race. (Warren Hokinson Collection)

Johnny Beauchamp is shown in his first roadster ride in 1949. Car owner Dale Swanson Sr. is shown with Beauchamp—this combination won a lot of Iowa roadster races. (Dale Swanson Jr. Collection)

Tiny Lund is shown with the car he drove in Iowa hot rod races. The photo was taken in 1949—probably at Pioneer Speedway in Des Moines. (Dale Swanson Jr. Collection)

This poster advertises races at the half-mile Harlan Fairgrounds track. The year is 1949. (Dale Swanson Jr. Collection)

The small town of Harlan in western Iowa has produced some good race drivers. It's per-capita yield of Daytona 500 winners is unmatched by any town anywhere. These Harlan natives are Johnny Beauchamp and Tiny Lund and both started their careers in the roadsters.

Beauchamp and Lund began racing in 1949. Both appeared in a roadster race at Hastings, Nebraska in the summer of that year. Beauchamp ran with the Central Iowa Roadster Association and the Hawkeye Hot Rod Racing Association, and was the winner of a main event at Kessell Speedway in Des Moines in 1950. Lund apparently quickly turned to stock car racing and Beauchamp followed suit in the early 1950s. Both moved on to the big time with NASCAR late model stock car racing.

Beauchamp's name is not on the books as a Daytona 500 winner. This was at the first 500-mile race on the then new Daytona Speedway. Beauchamp crossed the finish line in a "dead heat" with veteran driver, Lee Petty, and NASCAR took three days studying photos before declaring Petty the winner. Most racing historians now believe that Beauchamp was a lap ahead of Petty and was the true winner. Did NASCAR pull some strings to make sure a southern hero won the race and/or was their scoring less than perfect? Johnny Beauchamp died several years ago without credit for what was almost surely his greatest victory.

Tiny Lund was a long time NASCAR star and won the Daytona 500 in 1963. He was killed at Talladega, Alabama in 1975.

Cecil Maddox also drove this Vergil Thrasher car. This is at Guthrie Center in about 1950. (Elaine Higginson Collection)

Mort Mulford drove this street track hot rod in a few Iowa races. That is his future wife behind the wheel. (Mort Mulford Collection)

This is the Ed Parmenter Buick Eight at Marshalltown in about 1950. Parmenter ran fast in this car. (Lue Holland Collection)

Lue Holland had hit something very hard at an unknown Iowa track. Holland did far better in future races. (Lue Holland Collection)

Bob Kilfoil drove this car in Iowa roadster races. The engine appears to be some sort of a straight eight. (Lue Holland Collection)

A county fair horse track at Guthrie Center. That's Ed Parmenter winning a heat race. (Elaine Higginson Collection)

That's Doc Schaffer facing the camera. Schaffer raced roadsters in Nebraska and Iowa before moving to California to race sprint cars. (Elaine Higginson Collection)

Bobby VanHossen looks like the kid next door instead of the driver of #22. Van Hosen won a lot of Iowa roadster and midget races. (Alice VanHossen Collection)

Ed Parmenter's day at Guthrie Center came to an end with this crash. The engine is a Buick Eight—unusual in a track roadster. (Elaine Higginson Collection)

Bobby VanHossen drove this "California Style" track roadster. A nice looking car—assuming Van Hosen painted it. (Alice VanHossen Collection)

Kenny Higginson leads the pack at Carroll in 1950. Billy Richardson is in #4 as Jimmy Maddox hugs the pole under Wolheather in #44. (Elaine Higginson Collection)

Left–Lue Holland is pictured with his Ford V8 at Guthrie Center. Holland had a long and successful career in Midwest racing. (Elaine Higginson Collection)

Kenny Higginson is shown with car owner Bill Hillis. Higginson was successful in the roadsters, midgets and sprint cars. (Elaine Higginson Collection)

Kenny Higginson and Bill Hillis built this nice looking Iowa roadster. It is shown at Guthrie Center. (Elaine Higginson Collection)

This should be Pioneer Speedway in Des Moines. Bob Haeveland is on the pole in the Boyd Spiker Ford Six. (Elaine Higginson Collection)

The start of a heat race at Guthrie Center in about 1950. Speed Lyman is on the pole with Lue Holland on the outside. (Elaine Higginson Collection)

TRAGEDY AT COUNCIL BLUFFS

Playland Park at Council Bluffs was one of finest racing facilities In Iowa. Under the able promotion of Abe Shusky, the track drew near capacity crowds for the weekly midget races in 1949. Shusky wanted to try the roadsters and offered the same deal as the midgets-$1000 against 40% of the gate.

This was big money for the roadsters and the first race attracted a good field of cars from Iowa, Missouri and Nebraska. One of the drivers was Bill Pettit who had raced in California. During the feature Pettit tried to crowd between two cars and the fence, climbed a wheel and flipped end over end. He was dead when help reached him.

For the next week's races the sanction body, probably the Hawkeye Hot Rod Association, passed a rule requiring rollbars. Once again, a good field was on hand as well as a good crowd. The event may have been billed as a benefit for Bill Pettit. A new driver was Cyclone Ross—one of the few black racers. According to pre-race publicity he was sponsored by Joe Lewis and driving Tom Cherry's car from Indiana—it is doubtful if either was true. Ross got tangled up with two other cars in a heat race, flipped and slid to a stop upside down. He too died instantly. Ironically, the roll bar contributed to fatal head injuries.

This was enough for promoter Abe Shusky and the hot rods never again raced at Playland Park. The crashes were certainly no fault of the track or the drivers—just dreadful racing luck.

Lue Holland is shown in the car that earned him a Central Iowa Racing Association championship. (Lue Holland Collection)

CENTRAL IOWA
Hot Rod Association
MARSHALLTOWN, IOWA
This is to certify that:
Ma Brown
IS AN ASSOCIATE MEMBER IN GOOD STANDING
TO JAN. 1, 19__
Ed Parmenter
OWNER OR DRIVER SEC'Y-TREAS.
Good only in State of Iowa

This is a CIHRA card. It is not known who Ma Brown was. (Elaine Higginson Collection)

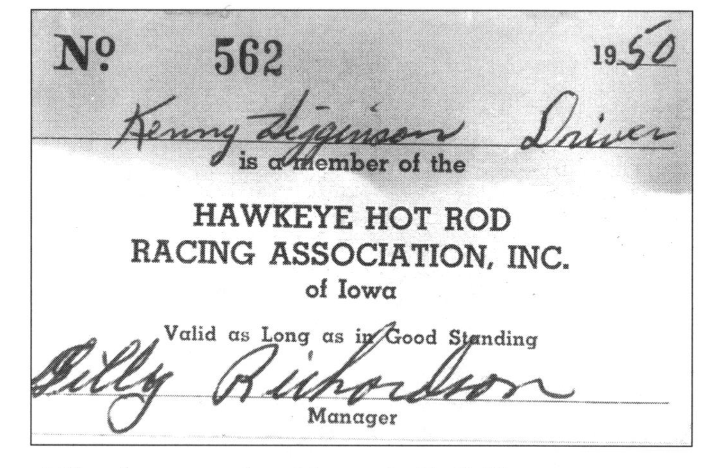
No 562 1950
Kenny Higginson Driver
is a member of the
HAWKEYE HOT ROD
RACING ASSOCIATION, INC.
of Iowa
Valid as Long as in Good Standing
Billy Richardson
Manager

A Hawkeye membership card. Both Kenny Higginson and Manager Billy Richardson were big names in Iowa racing. (Elaine Higginson Collection)

Action at Carroll on September 4, 1950. Kenny Higginson trails in #5. (Elaine Higginson Collection)

Kansas

Roadster racing in Kansas started in the 1930s when a series of races were held in various towns. The races were probably billed as stock car races but it is certain that most, or all, of the cars were stripped and modified roadsters. Kansas racing historian and *National Speed Sport News* writer, Emmett Carpenter, was one of the drivers who competed in these races.

During the post World War II roadster boom Kansas had more than it's share of roadster racing and at least six organizations were formed. The bulk of the racing was in the Wichita area at CeJay Stadium in that city and Jayhawk Speedway in Newton, some 30 miles north. Racing in this area started in 1947 with cars that could best be described as jalopies—some had no body behind the driver. These cars quickly evolved into true track roadsters. From mid-1947 until 1951, there was hot rod racing on a regular basis at CeJay and Jayhawk. Among the top Wichita roadster drivers were Charlie Lutkie, Bob Murra, Buddy Quick, Frankie Lies, and 1947 champion Jim Roper. (Roper later drove stock cars and was the winner of the first NASCAR race ever held—June 19, 1949 at Charlotte NC) The Wichita track also drew visitors from many states. From Texas came Bob Thorne and JD Hanna. One might expect nomadic Ken Stansberry to show up from California, and he did.

Roadster racing, at both Cejay and Jayhawk, was hit hard by the stock cars and was just about over by 1951. Surprisingly the roadsters were back in the late 1950s at 81 Speedway in north

This unidentified Oakley car looks like a cross between a roadster and sprint car but, odds are, that tail came from a '27 T.

Scott City and probably 1949. Most likely, there is a Chevy Six under the hood.

Action at Oakley in 1949. There is a good crowd on hand and the dust isn't too bad as Les Suter leads.

Nineteen forty-eight at Oakley. Jack Smith is on the pole with fellow Denver driver Rick Allen #34. Les Suter is on the outside of the second row.

Another unidentified High Plains Racing Association car. Looks like a Chevy.

Wichita—a track that still exists today. The roadsters were limited to six-cylinder overhead-valve engines or flathead V8s. This program lasted until about 1963 when the promoter allowed OHV V8s and the cars became supermodifieds.

Out in western Kansas there was a roadster group that, due to its remoteness, was very nearly forgotten. This was in Oakley and it was the High Plains Racing Association (HPRA). While not a large organization the HPRA made up in enthusiasm what it lacked in numbers. One of the early races (1948) at Oakley was held with only five cars and one of those was a Denver visitor. The *Oakley Graphic* reported that 1200 fans turned out on a hot, windy and dusty day and that "the racers gave them a good show" The newspaper goes on to report, "Jack Smith, car no. 8 of Denver brought a slick car which, literally fell to pieces during the races". Rough track? The purse that day was $362.50 and L.E. Pickrel won top honors and $140. The High Plains group, mostly under the leadership of Arnold "Blank" Blankenberg, ran races in Oakley and Scott City for several years. Top drivers were Les Suter, Bud Manning and eastern Kansas driver Frankie Lies. Visitors from other parts of Kansas and Colorado often supplemented the local cars. It is probable that the purses seldom exceeded $500.

In central Kansas, there was another roadster group that ran races at Dodge City, Dighton, Norton, Stockton, Plainville and WaKeeney. If this group had a name it has been forgotten but the promoter was Jack Merrick of Dodge City who went on to be one of the top race promoters in the state. The only known driver from this group was Troy Routh who drove Paul Hanke's Ardun V8 roadster. This car had very unusual quarter elliptic rear springs. Troy Routh turned up at a race on airport runways at Great Bend where he finished fourth and made $168.

All during the roadster era, there were occasional races on the legendary High Banks of Belleville—the same racetrack that still exists today. Most of the cars at the races were from nearby Nebraska although Wichita area and even some Oakley cars competed. Nebraska driver and current Indy USAC official, Andy Anderson won most of these races in the Merc powered "Belle of Belleville."

(Photos from the Punch Lemberg collection unless otherwise noted)

PUNCH

There were many ladies that worked behind the scene to support roadster racing. One of these was Margaret Suter Lemburg—better known as just plain "Punch." In most areas during the roadster years women were prohibited in the pits and, hence, could not actively participate. Punch took a very active part in High Plains events.

She was married to driver Les Suter and the two of them leased the track at Oakley for the races. Punch remembers that she did what was necessary to help with the races. "I was in the pits, in the announcers tower or, on occasion, drove a push truck. If we couldn't find a trophy girl I presented the trophy in my jeans."

Les Suter died in 1978 and Punch is now married to Ray Lemburg. The two of them are active in hot air balloon racing. All of the High Plains Racing Association photos are from the Punch Lemburg collection.

Punch Suter Lemburg "in uniform" and ready to go to work at a 1950 race in Oakley.

L.E. Pickrel drove this car. Photo is at Scott City and, from the looks of the Ford in the background, it is at least 1949.

Action at Scott City. Car #39 shows up in several photos but the driver's identity is not known.

This is the Jack Smith Merc from Denver. Looks like they are working on the "quick change" gearbox. Anybody remember those monsters?

Les Suter smiles for the camera—probably after winning a race at Oakley.

A mechanic works on the very low #74. Why the front rollbar? Perhaps to protect the driver if he went through one of those board fences?

Speed and More S-P-E-E-D
--AT THE--
AUTO RACES
Racing for the Championship of the Middlewest Auto Races
TWO BIG DAYS OF RACING AT THE
SCOTT COUNTY FAIR

An ad for the races at Scott City. Scott City and Oakley are about 50 miles apart and most of the HPRA events took place in these two towns.

The hot rods get ready to be pushed off for a race at Scott City

Les Suter in his Chevy Six. Suter later installed a Wayne head on this car.

This is the Les Suter car with the Wayne Chevy in place. Suter has made other modifications to create a very fast hot rod.

Melvin Widup of Hutchinson fielded this two-car team to race in Central Kansas. It is not known who drove the cars. (Donald Murphy Collection)

The Ricketts Chevrolet #22 was used as publicity for the Mickey Rooney racing epic, "The Big Wheel." It is hard to believe that this obviously heavy car won 14 features, but there is no definite evidence to prove otherwise.

EXTRA!

SEE THE FASTEST CAR IN WESTERN KANSAS

No. 22

A Chevrolet Hot Rod Racer, Owned by —
RICKETTS CHEVROLET CO., Winona, Kansas

Champion of High Plains Racing Circuit:
Scott City - Oakley - Goodland - Oberlin.

Winner of 14 Feature Races During 1950 Season.

On Display at Theatre During
Run of
"THE BIG WHEEL"

Sec. 35.66 P. L. & R.
U. S. POSTAGE
PAID
Holyrood, Kansas
Permit No. 2

Boxholder ....
Route ....

THE CHARM THEATRE

HOLYROOD, KANSAS

Left–Doc Schaffer drove this Merc at Belleville. (Lue Holland Collection)

Below–A rare front view of the "Belle of Belleville" roadster that won many races in Kansas and Nebraska. Cliff Clapper and Andy Anderson were among the drivers who posted victories in this car. (Lue Holland Collection)

Above–Bobby Van Hosen is shown at Belleville in 1950. (Lue Holland Collection)

Right–Frenchy Tyer gets ready to qualify at Belleville in about 1950. Owner Russ Stover is at the right. (Lue Holland Collection)

BLANK AND NUMBER 88

The hot Oldsmobile "88" overhead valve V8 came out in 1949. A few of these wound up in track roadsters but there is little doubt that Arnold "Blank" Blankenberg of Oakley was the first to use one in a hot rod. Blank pulled some strings to get one of the hard to find engines and then constructed a most unusual race car. Even though it ran with the roadsters, it wasn't a roadster. It wasn't a sprint car either—I guess "supermodified" would best describe it although that term wouldn't be around for ten or so years.

In the photos, the car appears unfinished but, so far as it is known, the car ran in that configuration for several years. For an unknown reason, Blankenberg mounted the radiator in the rear. Perhaps this was to help balance the weight of the heavy engine? The engine was near stock but was certainly faster than most of the competition. Bud Manning was the very brave pilot of this machine and drove it to a number of victories. Manning finished fifth at the Great Bend 100 miler and timed third fastest at a Belleville event. That car on that track? A fearless man indeed!

Driver Bud Manning and owner, Blank Blankenberg are pictured at an Oakley race in about 1950.

Bud Manning celebrates a victory at a Kansas track. He sits high and VERY exposed in the Blankenberg Olds 88.

Driver Bud Manning gets ready for a race someplace in Kansas.

Michigan

A form of roadster racing started in Michigan as early as 1926 when "hobo" races were held in several locations. Owen Granger took part in these races and won a lot of them in his four cylinder Chevy. The competing cars were no doubt stripped roadsters (just how far they were stripped is not known) and hopped up engines were allowed. Information from Granger's son, O.B., indicates that the races paid, at best, $50 to win.

Additional evidence of roadster racing comes

Whiskey Ridge promoter Jack Fiske owned this car and Dick Peoples drove it. Fiske also used it to haul groceries to his cabin in the woods. (Julie Fiske Collection)

George Smith in an early Whiskey Ridge car. Looks like a very much cutdown Chevy.

This is either Ray Wilde or "Nelson" plowing through the loose Whiskey Ridge dirt.

Art Thomas bounces along in an early Whiskey Ridge race. For a time there were two classes at the track—four cylinder and eight cylinder.

from an entry blank for races at Jackson on September 9, 1934. The printed rules are a bit vague but it does sound like a roadster race. Part of the entry blank reads, "All cars must be stripped for racing and carry a hood." The promoters were not bashful and billed the race as a "National Championship." The advertised purse was $299 with $100 to win the 15 mile main event. In addition to the purse there were, "Loving cups and throphies (sic) to the winners." Looks like the tobacco industry was involved too as entries were to be mailed to the Riverside Cigar Store in Jackson. Certainly, dozens of races like this took place in Michigan in the 1930s.

After World War II, roadster racing became much more organized and at least three roadster groups were formed. These were the Michigan Racing Association, the Michigan Modified Stock Car Association and (another) Michigan Racing Association by Indiana and Michigan racers. Much of the racing was at Saginaw on a modified horse track. The roadsters also took to the high banks of Owosso when that track opened in 1946. Races were also held at Kalamazoo, Grand Rapids, Marne, Muskegon and Allegan. Later on, there was a successful series of races held at Parkington's Pastures near Detroit. The roadsters also appeared intermittently at Andy Barto's Detroit Motor Speedway.

Among the better Michigan hot rod drivers were Joe Quinn, Matt Heid, Gervasise Umek, Hod Preston, future Indy driver Al Miller and Iggy Katona who went on to fame in the stock cars.

Much of Michigan's roadster history was written at the racetrack "out in the boonies" east of Muskegon. The track with the wonderful name of Whiskey Ridge. At the beginning, in 1946, both the track and the cars were primitive beyond belief. Racing started on a rough and tumble off road course with bumps, hills and gullies. As the years went on the track was improved and some very good racecars and drivers competed at Whiskey Ridge. It seems that there were few, if any, rules at Whiskey Ridge and, so far as is known, no organized group was formed there. Pete Spencer ran his very fast Chevy Six sprint car there on occasion. One of the best track roadsters in the country, the California Roadster Association Burt Letner #19 Merc, showed up at least one Whiskey Ridge race. A tribute to some of the rough appearing Whiskey Ridge cars is that the car (probably with Red Amick driving) did not win that day.

This chapter is pretty well overloaded with Whiskey Ridge photos. There were some amazing cars that raced there—enjoy!

Unless noted all Whiskey Ridge photos are from the collection of Michigan racing historian Nelson Wierenga of Grand Rapids.

A four abreast start in 1946. Looks like the white car is a hastily stripped street machine.

Ray Wilde gets a tow in 1946. Note the highly advanced traction device strapped to the rear crossmember.

This must be late 1946 and Whiskey Ridge is nearer to an oval track. Ray Flanery is on the outside in a Plymouth.

THE RIVER ROAD JALOPY TRACK

The racing at the River Road Jalopy Track, in Grand Haven, was typical of a dozen or a hundred tracks all over the country in the years immediately following WW II. The track was primitive, the cars were rough versions of track roadsters, the fields and crowds were small and the drivers mostly locals.

George Shippers ran the River Road track and from him comes this story of typical minor league roadster racing. The track opened in 1946 as a semi-off road course. There was no organization formed and very few rules. About the only obvious rule was that only open cars were permitted. Most cars were "constructed" by cutting down whatever car was handy until it was deemed fit to race. It was OK to use V8 engines in Model As but all engines were supposed to be stock.

When asked if there was a possibility that some cheating went on Shippers replied, "They all cheated!"

Racing went on at River Road until 1948 and the racetrack became a half mile oval. The cars also evolved into much better racecars. Some of the better drivers at River Road were Tom Suspenski, Tony Tragna, Art Thomas and Joe Bisocky. The latter two are familiar Whiskey Ridge names.

All the River Road Jalopy Track photos are from the collection of George Shippers. It appears that the photos were taken in 1946. There are no driver identifications and some photos have been damaged.

Even if it were stock this, lightweight Ford V8 would be a fairly fast car.

The builder of #99 went to considerable trouble with the tail of that car. Bodywork is a bit rough.

A cutdown Model A leads the field on what appears to be a very sandy track.

No helmet and no firewall but that chrome radiator shell is nice.

Car #201 has an unusual design but is well constructed. Probably a high dollar sponsorship.

"Bud" built one of the nicer looking River Road cars.

Del Dempsey roars around Whiskey Ridge in a very stripped V8. Looks like there is no seat belt but is it more dangerous for Dempsey or for the unprotected spectators?

Harry Wilke skirts this tangle in the Whiskey Ridge dust. Car #100 is Rance Stevens, the second driver is unknown and Joe Bisocky is driving the third car.

FIGURE THIS ONE OUT!

There were a few rear-engined roadsters built and a fair amount of information is available on some of them. Harvey Ward built a rear-engined car and ran at Whiskey Ridge. This car is a real puzzle. Attempts have been made to find Ward or his family but without success. Harvey Ward is certainly to be admired for having the courage and ingenuity to try something different. It also took a lot of courage to drive that machine!

It is certain that Ward started with a Ford chassis. It is equally certain that he had cooling problems. Beyond that it is guesswork and your guess is as good as mine is.

Both photos are from the Paul Weisner-Nelson Wierenga Collection.

Below–It looks like something has broken on the Ward machine. Here the radiator is in an upright position and Ward has built a nose for the car. What is that at the rear of the car? Another radiator? Another engine? Wish that guy would move his head!

Harvey Ward is shown in his rear-engined car at Whiskey Ridge—probably 1948. Is there any rear suspension? What is under that rear-tilting radiator?

Vern Johnson kicks up a lot of dirt. His #15 is an Essex.

Car #0 loses a wheel as Billy Moore tries to do the right thing. Flying wheels were another hazard for Whiskey Ridge spectators.

The lineup at a 1947 race. Bill Circa is in #49, #9 is unknown, Larry Howe is in #1 and that's Gene Allen at the right.

A mixed field gropes through the Whiskey Ridge dust. The photo was probably taken from the judge's stand.

This is "Hells Turn"—a 30 foot unprotected drop-off. Harry Wilke is on the pole with Rance Stevens on the outside.

A not uncommon tangle at Whiskey Ridge. Larry Howe is spinning out—Vern Johnson is at the right in Lloyd Rockey's car.

Gene Farber runs to the aid of flagman Art Carrier after he hit him with his Caddie V8 roadster. Carrier was severely hurt but came out of it OK.

Tim Parketon in Larry Howe's car. This is a cut-down and modified—-something?

Track attendants work to clear a Whiskey Ridge crash. Perhaps there is an injured driver in the background. Larry Howe's car is at the left and #8 is either Joe Crane or Art Thomas.

The odd shape of Whiskey Ridge comes from it's origins as an off road course. There is another excellent crowd on hand.

An unidentified driver is all crossed up as he takes the flag from starter Jackie Robinson.

Dick Peoples spins out of a 1946 race at Whiskey Ridge. Peoples went on to become a fine roadster, sprint car and stock car driver—and he bought a helmet!

Two cars crash in the dust. Judging from the photos, most of the time Whiskey Ridge was near dust free.

Probably 1948. Glen Rockey is on the outside in the #11 roadster and that's Robert Harrah at the right.

THE TALE OF THE BROWN DOG

For track roadsters to have an animal nickname was not unusual. There was a rat, a pig or a dog. All were uncomplimentary and all depicted a slow and/or ugly racecar. Not so with Hod Preston. He called his car "The Brown Dog" and did so affectionately.

Hod Preston had a couple of years experience in racing when he built what was pretty much a typical track roadster. The car had a Model A frame, a '27 Model T body and a Mercury engine with the normal hot rod goodies. It was a "working" racecar with no fancy frills. Hod painted the car a flat army brown color—one has to think he got the paint for nothing or maybe very cheap at a military surplus store. This did little to enhance the car's very ordinary appearance. With Preston at the wheel, the car ran fast and was a winner at numerous tracks in the Midwest.

It was a fan from Hicksville, Ohio who provided the cars nickname by remarking that the car, "Ran like hell, but looked like a scroungy brown dog." Hod overheard the remark and had to admit it was true. Preston, a bit of a showman, went along with the fan's observations and promptly painted "Brown Dog" on the side of the car.

Preston and The Brown Dog won races at Michigan tracks such as Owosso and Saginaw. At Saginaw Hod showed a definite lack of showmanship when he and The Brown Dog dispatched the entire field of nine cars in one lap of an Australian Pursuit race.

It was at Detroit's Motor City Speedway on May 30, 1949 that Preston and The Brown Dog enjoyed a very good night and a very good payoff. Promoter Andy Barto usually ran the AAA midgets, but with many of the top drivers in Indianapolis for the Memorial Day weekend Barto was faced with a lack of cars. On short notice he scheduled the roadsters—in Detroit they were billed as "Modified Stock Cars." The fans responded by turning out in record numbers and contributed to a gate of over $8000. Preston and The Brown Dog had fast time, won the dash, a heat race and the main event for a payoff of $422.

It would be nice to say that The Brown Dog was retired to a life of ease but, like most roadsters, it just sort of disappeared as the parts were used on other racecars. Preston moved on to other types of racing and later into promotions. Hod got along well with the racers, the press and the fans. He was an innovator and among the first to bring racing to the TV screens in the Detroit area. Hod Preston had learned some of the elements of showmanship from "The Brown Dog."

Name H. Preston Date 5/30/49

EVENT POS. PURSE RECEIVED OF —

MOTOR CITY SPEEDWAY, INC.

$ 39 00
$ 39 00
$ 32 00
$ 312
$ 422 00

TOTAL $ Hod Preston Driver's Signature

A very nice payoff! Very few roadster drivers ever won this much—maybe not even in a career. (Eustice Preston Collection)

Hod Preston at Saginaw in 1949. His well built "Brown Dog" had no unnecessary frills. (Paul Weisner Collection)

Inset–Matt Heid drove this very fast Ford Six in Michigan roadster races. He was killed in this car at Owosso in 1948. (Weisner-Wierenga Collection)

One of the most famous roadsters in the country at Whiskey Ridge in 1949. The Bert Letner Mercury from California. (Weisner-Wierenga Collection)

A good view of Whiskey Ridge. The photo was taken from the edge of "Hells Turn." (Julie Fiske Collection)

Here is one way to get some inside weight. Rance Stevens strapped a head from a Caddie flathead V8 to the left rear of his car.

A dusty day at Whiskey Ridge. That's Matt Heid on the outside in third place. (Weisner-Wierenga Collection)

This is probably Red Amick qualifying at Whiskey Ridge. Both the Letner #19 and Amick won lots of races but not on this day. (Weisner-Wierenga Collection)

The Pete Spencer Chevy sprint car at Whiskey Ridge. The car was allowed to run with the roadsters. (Weisner-Wierenga Collection)

HOT ROD DRIVERS!

The Michigan Modified Stock Auto Racing Association

Invites You to Race At

MOTOR CITY SPEEDWAY

JUNE 28th

Time trials 6:45 — Races at 8.30

OPEN COMPETITION

ALL ASSOCIATIONS WELCOME!

Contact: HOD PRESTON, Business Mgr.

5200 Tarnow Avenue Detroit 10, Michigan

Phone: VInewood 17340

Above–Driver Hod Preston helped out with the promotion of Michigan Roadsters. This is probably 1951. (Eustice Preston Collection)

Marne in about 1947. Larry Howe gets ready to start in his unusual roadster. (Wierenga Collection)

Above–This is Galesburg in 1949. Red Newman swept the program in this Owen Granger Merc. (O.B. Granger Collection)

Gene Farber at Whiskey Ridge. Farber and #272 won many Michigan roadster races. (Weisner-Wierenga Collection)

Minnesota

The only information on prewar Minnesota roadster racing comes from an ad by the Clements Chevrolet Company in Rochester. It tells of a 1928 Chevy roadster winning a "Jollopy Derby." Surely, there was more than one race held and surely, the cars were a form of track roadster.

Like elsewhere, post-war Minnesota roadster racing began with mostly street hot rods. This was in the spring of 1947 and the first race was at Farmington, near Minneapolis. It appears that the racing in 1947 was under the sanction of the Mid West Racing Association. In October of 1947, an attempt was made to run a major 50-lap race at the Minnesota State Fairgrounds track in Minneapolis. The race was pretty much of a bust as poor officiating and overheating cars contributed to a less than crowd pleasing race.

Chevrolet Wins Again

From the Junk Pile to the Jollopy Derby
1928 Chevrolet Comes Through

[illegible] GRUELLING LAPS TO WIN. NO ADDED OIL OR WATER.

YOU CAN BUY A USED CAR HERE THAT WILL GIVE SERVICE

DELUXE CHEVROLET SEDAN	OLDSMOBILE 6 CYLINDER TOURING SEDAN	FORD V8 TOURING SEDAN	DELUXE PLYMOUTH COUPE
STANDARD CHEVROLET COUPE	FORD V8 TUDOR	DELUXE CHEVROLET COACH	STANDARD CHEVROLET COACH

Clements Chevrolet Co.

This photo is the total extent of the known prewar roadster history in Minnesota. The "Jollopy Derby" was held at the Olmsted County Fairgrounds in Rochester. (Hoot Gibson Collection)

Harvey Porter ran a series of successful #4R cars. This is the first one in 1947. (Harvey Porter Collection)

An early roadster race at Albert Lea. This was before there was a roadster organization in Minnesota. (Dick Postier Collection)

The roadsters get ready to start at Farmington. Harvey Porter is on the pole, Art Bailey is in #7 and Tommy Adelman in #111—all were great roadster drivers. (Harvey Porter Collection)

Farmington in 1947. Harvey Porter is in a "new" #4R car. No identification on the driver of #44. (Harvey Porter Collection)

This is Vern Kolb's first track roadster—obviously a converted street rod. (Vern Kolb Collection)

In 1948, the Minnesota Roadster Racing Association (MRRA) was formed and this group pretty well dominated racing in the state. Most of the racing was in the Minneapolis-St. Paul area at Farmington and Rex Speedways. There was also racing at a number of county fair horse tracks at towns like Albert Lea, Duluth, Faribault, Owatonna, Kasson and St. Cloud.

There was another Minnesota organization—Gopher Racing Inc. and promoter Hoot Gibson probably owned it. Gopher ran the hot rods at Rochester, Austin and St. Charles.

Crowds at Rex Speedway were regularly reported at 5000 or over so the MRRA drivers enjoyed payoffs that were far above the roadster average. The purses at Rex Speedway probably averaged around $1000 and were perhaps half that at Farmington. Harvey Porter kept track of his winnings in 1948 and racked up a total of $2400 in 26 races. Neil Arndt banked $1700 as his (50%) drivers share in 28 races. Both Porter and Arndt were top drivers but other racers enjoyed good payoffs too.

In 1949 Twin Cities Speedway opened in the metropolitan Minneapolis-St Paul area and a feud developed between this track and the well-established Rex Speedway. Drivers who chose to race at Twin Cities were barred from MRRA events. This split in the ranks apparently did not last very long and, at least, did not destroy roadster racing as in other areas.

Most Minnesota cars ran the conventional Ford or Merc V8s but there were some successful "oddballs." The Vern Tritten's big Buick Straight Eights were winners—both on the track and in (lack of) beauty. Nobody argued with the fact that Tritten's Buicks were flat ugly! Dick Postier ran an OHV Nash Six that performed very well. In 1952 Harvey Porter switched from a Merc to a Four Port Riley Model B based engine and went very fast.

Drivers Tommy Adelmann, Al Lowrie, Harvey Porter and Carl Souvie are recorded as winning championships in Minnesota. Other top drivers were Art Bailey, Neil Arndt, Speed Chamberlain, Frank Zurckey, Dick Postier, Vern Kolb, Howie Hoffman, Red Grant, Bernie Wehner and Harold Burns.

George Anderson is shown in his flathead Model B. A very neat car. (George Anderson Collection)

Rex Speedway in Minneapolis in 1948. Vern Kolb is kicking up dirt on the outside and Frank Zrucky hugs the pole in his Buick. (Vern Kolb Collection)

Pete Beatty of Owatonna drove this car. The engine is probably a big Buick Eight. The MRRA had no limit on engine displacement. (George Anderson Collection)

Al Lowrie in promoter Hoot Gibson's car. Engine type? Check that hand brake and those knobby tires. (Hoot Gibson Collection from Dave Norgaarden)

Dick Postier's Nash Six is a contender for the "Most Dangerous Hot Rod" honors? Today, Postier admits, "My body served as the rollbar." Fortunately, he didn't try it out. (Dick Postier Collection)

Vern Kolb is about to get a very small trophy at Farmington in 1948. Kolb and his friend, Bernie Wehner, co-owned a number of cars and the "WK" was usually on the front nerf bar. (Vern Kolb Collection)

Jerry Arndt in a Buick Straight Eight at Rex Speedway in 1948. Half a dozen Buicks ran with MRRA—this is probably the best looking. (Neil Arndt Collection)

Action at Farmington. Neil Arndt in one of the Vern Tritten Buicks leads Vern Kolb. (Vern Kolb Collection)

Great action at Rex Speedway in about 1949. Neal Arndt in #1 1/2 as Harvey Porter is all crossed up on the outside. That's Tom Adelman in #11 and Les Mussel on the pole. (Harvey Porter Collection)

Harvey Porter at New Brighton in 1948. That front bumper very nicely serves as a wing! Harvey Porter Collection)

Herman Beede built the Buick Eight. Carl Souvie drove it at Farmington. (Carl Souvie Collection)

More action at Rex. Harvey Porter leads with Bernie Wehner close behind in #72 and Ed Bailey in #76. That guy wire looks a bit hazardous. (Harvey Porter Collection)

Art Bailey drove his own Cadillac V8 in a few races in 1950. The car was not successful. (Neil Arndt Collection)

THE TRITTEN BUICKS AND NEIL ARNDT

There were not too many track roadsters built with the monstrous 320 cubic inch Buick Straight Eight engines for power plants. (Most roadster associations allowed a maximum 300 cubic inches engine displacement. This worked out fine as most builders used the Mercury V8s which, with (normal) maximum boring and stroking, came out to 296 cubic inches. (Cheater Mercs of up to 340 cubic inches are rumored to have existed)

Neil Arndt and the Buick in 1996. Arndt has aged handsomely but #1 1/2 has definitely found the Fountain of Youth—in Dave Norgaarden's shop! (Neil Arndt Collection)

A rare photo of Vern Tritten who always wore those bib overalls and a straw hat. He is shown with Neil Arndt after a Minnesota roadster race. (Neil Arndt Collection)

The Minnesota Roadster Racing Association had no maximum engine displacement limit. Most cars still used Merc V8s but Vern Tritten built two cars with huge Buick engines. Tritten earned a living by grinding feed for farmers. His mobile rigs used home built Buick Straight Eight engines for power—lots of power! The Buicks were bored to 357 cubic inches, had 10.25 to 1 compression ratio, a Winfield super cam grind and double Buick oil pumps that put out 60 psi. Most of Tritten's business was in the winter so the full house engines would be well broken in on the feed grinders and then go in the racecars in the spring. Tritten's cars were crude and rough but, with those big Buicks. (they surely had 100 more horsepower than the opposition.)

Tritten built the Buicks (# 1 1/2 and #1 3/4) in 1948 and the cars were raced for several years. Al

Today, Neil Arndt wonders, (in his words) "Bad luck or bad driving?" (Neil Arndt Collection)

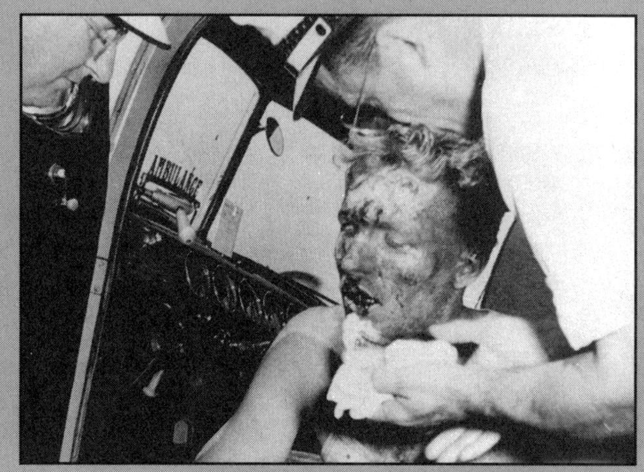

Lowrie, in one of the Buicks, reportedly won 29 of 32 main events in 1948 and was MRRA champion in 1949 and 1950. A list of Tritten's drivers is also far from complete but they include Lowrie, Art Bailey, Harold Burns and Neil Arndt. For Neil Arndt the Tritten Buicks were pretty much his "regular rides"—especially the #1 1/2 car.

Arndt drove the Buicks very well and was con-

This is 1950—Neil Arndt in the Tritten Buick. A brave man indeed to drive this car! (Dave Norgaarden Collection)

sidered Vern Tritten's top driver—he was paid 50% of the purses instead of the normal 40%. (As the photos indicate, he also had some crashes. The NASCAR hotshots also crash but not in Tritten Buicks!)

Arndt remembers his finest day of racing on September 10, 1950 at Don Voge's Twin Cities Speedway. The track was more than "tacky"—Neil still remembers the sucking sound of the knobby tires pulling out of the clay. It was a track made for the big Buick and Arndt took full advantage of it. He easily swept the program for a payoff of $220—Arndt and Tritten split a big stack of dollar bills.

Neil Arndt moved on to other types of racing and, after the roadster era, the Tritten Buicks were retired. One of them still exists and was recently found and restored by Dave Norgaarden of Rochester, Minnesota. This is the #1 1/2 car that Arndt drove to so many victories. Norgaarden graciously sold the car to Neil for a remarkably small sum so the two "old friends" are together again. Arndt is running the Buick in IMCA old-timers events and is having a ball reliving the past.

Art Bailey looks like he is recovering from a spin as Harvey Porter goes by in #4R. Bailey was killed in the # 1 3/4 Buick on June 22, 1950. (Harvey Porter Collection)

Harvey Porter is in a low slung Buick powered car in the Rex Speedway photo. That's Red Grant in #25 on the outside. (Harvey Porter Collection)

Al Lowrie shows off his trophies for winning the 1950 MRRA championship. He was one of several very good drivers who drove the Tritten Buicks. (Hoot Gibson Collection)

Right–Carl Souvie drove this neat DeSoto Six at Rex Speedway in 1950. The engine was more than a match for the V8s. (Carl Souvie Collection)

Left–Dick Postier built and drove this Nash Six in 1949. Postier worked for a Nash agency and liked the rugged construction and good low-end torque of the Nash engine. (Dick Postier Collection)

Heavy traffic at Rex. Left to right is Jerry Arndt, Neil Arndt, Red Grant, Harvey Porter, Howie Hoffman, Dane Tellie and Ray Bailey. (Harvey Porter Collection)

Action at the Austin Fairgrounds in 1950. Tom Adelman leads, Carl Souvie is in #D2, Harvey Porter in 73 and Bernie Wehner in #72. (Carl Souvie Collection)

Carl Souvie on his way to setting a track record at Rex Speedway. The car is the Don Shogmo Four Port Riley—a sprint car chassis. (Carl Souvie Collection)

A RILEY OHV V8

There is only one known Riley OHV Ford V8 that ever ran in track roadster competition. It wound up in Minnesota.

George Riley was a legend in the racing world and speed equipment built or designed by him has been around since the 1920s. This remarkable man manufactured carburetors, both flathead and OHV units for the Model A or B Ford and was closely involved with the fabulous Novi at Indianapolis.

One of George Riley's lesser known projects was an overhead valve conversion for the Ford V8. This was a sorely needed product, as it would allow the engine to breathe much more freely as well as solving the chronic overheating problem. The Riley units were designed for the 1937 Ford V8—this was the first engine with the water pumps in the block but it still had the early 21-stud heads. In 1938, Ford went to a 24-stud head and the design remained that way until the last flathead in 1953. For unknown reasons (probably at least partly financial) Riley never updated his OHV heads to the 24-stud configuration. The cost of the heads is unknown—around $200 would be good guess and nobody knows how many units were produced. Suffice it to say they were and are rare.

The Riley engine that wound up in Minnesota started life in a dry lakes car in California. It was owned by William Roberts and ran (probably with a streamliner body) at Rosamond Dry Lake at a speed of 149 MPH. In April of 1951, it was sold to Eugene Kutschier who converted the car to a track roadster. The car was apparently raced in Southern California until the owner moved to St. Paul in 1953. Wayne Allison who was also a part owner of the car drove the car at Twin Cities Speedway.

No record of the cars performance on the track has turned up. It does not appear in any of about 1000 Southern California photos on file nor in the hundred or so Minnesota photos available. The engine was small, at 225 cubic inches, but it should have been competitive in either California or Minnesota. It must be assumed that the car was just not raced very often.

Perhaps because the engine was so rare the car survived and did not just disappear, as did so many track roadsters. A few years ago Dave Norgaarden and Harvey Porter acquired the car and have restored it. The car has been exhibited and run at Knoxville, Iowa and other Midwest vintage meets.

Wayne Allison in the Riley OHV roadster at Twin Cities Speedway in 1953. Was the car raced that day? Allison's dirty face indicates he has been in competition but the car is too clean and why is it hooked to the tow bar? (Harvey Porter Collection)

The Riley Overhead Valve V8 in 1992. The two Stromberg carburetors were probably not original equipment. (Dave Norgaarden Collection)

Knoxville, Iowa in 1992. Dave Norgaarden is shown with the beautiful Riley roadster that he and Harvey Porter restored. (Harvey Porter Collection)

Ray Klabunder sends dirt flying as he chases Carl Souvie in #70. This is Twin Cities Speedway. (Carl Souvie Collection)

Left–Glen Anderson was the driver of this Merc powered roadster. Apparently, Anderson had no superstitions about the number 13. (George Anderson Collection)

Bernie Wehner poses for the cameraman after a win someplace in Minnesota. (Bernie Wehner Collection)

Harold Burns crashes hard at Rex Speedway. He was OK except for minor cuts. The photo is from Racing Wheels Magazine. (Carl Souvie Collection)

More action at Rex—no wonder the track drew big crowds. Harold Burns is on the pole in an Olds 88 V8. Harvey Porter crowds him in #4R as Wayne Allison sticks to the outside. (Harvey Porter Collection)

Left–Carl Souvie in the Olds 88. The Rex Backer owned machine was heavy, hard to steer and, despite lots of horsepower, not very successful. (Carl Souvie Collection)

Right–A couple of DeSotos in action at Twin Cities Speedway in 1952. Les Mussel is on the pole in the six banger and Ray Klabunder in the Hemi-V8 on the outside. Bob Doyscher owned both cars and the #D2 ran in the 1953 "Little 500" at Anderson, Indiana. With West Coast ace, Johnny Key, at the wheel it finished a close second in the long grind. (Carl Souvie Collection)

Carl Souvie cranks out a fast lap at St Cloud in about 1950. The #32 Don Shogmo Four Port Riley often beat the V8s. (Carl Souvie Collection)

Right–Harvey Porter drove this Four-Port Riley. The car appears to be quite short—the MRRA rule on wheelbase read simply, "Optional." (Harvey Porter Collection)

Missouri

Roadster racing in Missouri probably started in Smithville on May 24, 1931 with an exhibition run by a Riley equipped Model A. Vic Damon drove a street roadster and set "a new state record."

From the mid-1930s to 1942, roadster races were held at a dozen or so Missouri towns. It is most likely that some of the races were billed as "Hobo" or "Junk Car Races." These cars were stripped to a bare frame—no body—just a seat for the driver. Engine modifications were permitted, so these were basically track roadsters (or big cars) with no bodies. The then common Model T, Model A-B and Chevy Four engines were the most popular but other makes did run. The lightweight machines must have been quite fast and, certainly, were very dangerous. It no doubt varied around the state but some cars acquired roadster bodies as time went on. A big purse would be $200 with about $50 to the winner. Among the towns where this racing took place were South Kansas City, Smithville, Dodson and Paris.

Paris in the 1930s. A couple of Hobo drivers get ready for a race. No seat belt and no helmet for the driver of #33 (Ruby Cortright Collection)

After the war racing resumed at Springfield in 1947. Quite possibly, these were some of the left over "Junk Cars." Future racing great, Junior Hower drove his street hot rod from Kansas City to race at Springfield. To his surprise, he found a full field of cars stripped to the frame—lightweight and track proven machines. Hower's A-V8 was no match for these cars and he started an illustrious racing career by finishing last. It is not known what happened to this Springfield racing group and that this is the only evidence of roadster racing in that city.

The more formal Missouri roadster racing started later in 1947 at Smithville, Hopkins, St Joseph and at Heart of America Speedway near Kansas City. The Mid West Hot Rod Association was formed and, in 1948, the Pony Express Racing Association and a little known Tri States Hot Rod Circuit.

Some of the Missouri cars started life as street roadsters, but by 1948, most of the hot rods were pure racecars. For the next couple of years there was some good roadster racing in half a dozen Missouri towns. The wining drivers included Hi Flashing, Herschel Wagner, Pat Cunningham, Tom DeVolter, Johnny Tatlock, Scotty Scoville and Junior Hower who won the Mid West Hot Rod Association title several times. The Kansas City area also attracted many visitors—historian Ray Boyles has documented 120 drivers who raced in the Kansas City area hot rod races.

A little data is available on the purses at Missouri roadster races. Most were small—less than $500. There were some races at Riverside Stadium in Kansas City and purses should have been larger there.

A most unusual roadster. This the Lyle Fine car at Hopkins in 1948. It is doubtful if the Lincoln V-12 was competitive. (Ray Boyles Collection)

There is a good crowd on hand for this race at Paris in the 1930s. Note the total lack of protection for spectators. (Ruby Cortright Collection)

Junior slides inside of Johnny Tatlock. This is Heart of America Speedway near Kansas City in 1947. (Ray Boyles Collection)

A very varied field of Hobo cars gets ready for a Paris race. The make of #7 is unknown but it looks POWERFUL! (Ruby Cortright Collection)

MISSOURI ROADSTER RACING 1937

The following is from a letter written by Ray Eaton of Payette Idaho.

"I was never involved too much with the roadsters. While living in Kansas City, in about 1937, a small group of us wild ones did run a few dusty tracks. I recall a friend and I built a "29 Model A roadster, Riley flathead, Winfield carb, low speed rear end and knobby rear tires. We towed it to Paris Missouri for a race. Upon arrival, the promoter met us with the good news. He was short of cars and paying customers. If we would run, after the race, we could have all the fried chicken and beer we could hold.

"I wouldn't call it a race, about six cars floundered around in the dust, making a lot of noise, we would pass and repass for a show for the few paying customers. Everyone was happy."

In the next race, at Dodson, Eaton hit a dirt bank and broke his nose. He moved on to wrenching for some very good IMCA big cars. Later, in Arizona, he promoted a few races and, recently, has built some replica vintage sprint cars.

This is Savannah in 1951. A good field of cars from both Missouri and Iowa are on hand. (Elaine Higginson Collection)

The hot rods line up at Savannah in 1951. The driver of car #5 is Kenny Higginson from Iowa. (Elaine Higginson Collection)

Jim Ruth clowns with his crew after winning a Savannah race. Ruth was a regular with the CRA in California and a visitor in Missouri. (Jim Ruth Collection)

A car goes over the bank at Savannah. The driver's identity is uncertain but Scotty Scoville usually drove the #99 Four Port Riley. (Elaine Higginson Collection)

A poor photo of an interesting Missouri car. This is the Paul Hanke Ardun-Merc V8. Troy Routh is the driver. (Barclay Collection)

Herschel Wagner at heart of America Speedway in 1947. The "W" on the bumper is for owner Kenny Welch. (Ray Boyles Collection)

Herschel Wagner in the Roy Thomas Hilligass Offy at the Oklahoma State Fairgrounds. Just compare the beautiful lines of this machine with today's squashed and boxy sprint cars—progress? (Leroy Byers Collection)

Herschel Wagner is best known as an IMCA sprint car driver. He won a lot of races on this circuit of rough fairgrounds racetracks and big Offys. Wagner got his start in the roadsters—his memory of what happened nearly 60 years ago is remarkably good.

It was probably around 1935 when Wagner started racing. This was in South Kansas City at a completely forgotten track called Benjamini Ranch. His first car was a "Junk Car"—a Model T with a Fronty head stripped to the bare frame. He doesn't remember how he did or how much he won other than, "Not much, but a dollar was a dollar then."

In other races Wagner drove four cylinder Chevies, Durants, a big overweight Marmon and even a V8—an Oakland V8 that is. He remembers Missouri tracks at Smithville, Dodson and South Kansas City. There was Olathe, Kansas and even trips to Iowa, Illinois and Oklahoma. The purses at these far-flung tracks would be $200 to $300 on a good day.

At one point he had his own roadster—actually a pickup. It was an open Model A pickup that he used to deliver coal during the week. On race days, the bed came off and it was Wagner's racecar.

Herschel Wagner drove roadsters after the war in Missouri but soon switched to the IMCA sprint cars. He campaigned on that circuit for many years. He survived the junk car-roadster days with only a few bumps and bruises but was very seriously injured in a sprint car crash at Shreveport, Louisiana.

Herschel Wagner lives in Kansas City, Missouri and has recently celebrated his 80th birthday.

N. Carolina

There was a limited amount of roadster racing in North Carolina. No information is available on prewar racing but logically there was the same type of Jalopy-Junk Car-Roadster racing that went on in many states.

It appears that a stock car or modified stock car program got going in North Carolina before World War II and this was resumed after the war. Hence, roadster racing faced competition from the beginning. It is believed there were roadster races at Salisbury, Shelby, Charlotte and Raleigh. Despite intensive research, nothing on these races has turned up.

The only actual documentation on North Carolina roadster racing comes from Dot Gladis of Port Orange, Florida. Dot Gladis was a very successful modified stock car driver in the early 1950s and competed on an even basis with the top male drivers of that time. Gladis also drove roadsters and along with another lady, Nellie Higgins, ran in a roadster race at High Point in June of 1950. Unfortunately, no results of that race are available, nor are photos.

A newspaper clipping for the 1950 High Point race, sent by Dot Gladis, mentioned the roadsters were "Charlotte's band of hot rod drivers." Drivers listed were Mickey Fenn, Bill Wildenhouse, Jack Owens and Jack Thompson. Fenn and Wildenhouse were reported as recent winners of races at Elkin and Wadesboro. Obviously, there was a roadster group in Charlotte and they were reasonably active. It is sad that so little has been found out about this chunk of racing history.

Nebraska

Like in many other states, there must have been roadster racing in Nebraska in the 1930s. Like in many other states, no information is available.

After the war, it took awhile for roadster racing to get going in Nebraska. The first races were at Hastings late in 1948 and, that winter, the Nebraska Hot Rod Racing Association (NHRRA) was formed. In 1949 racing began on a regular basis and for the next several years, the NHRRA raced about once a week on a dozen or more tracks throughout Nebraska. Races were held at Hastings, Beatrice, North Platte, Broken Bow, Wahoo, York, Fairbury, Holdrege, Franklin, Osceola, Nelson, Ord and at Pioneer Speedway in Omaha. With the exception of Ord and Pioneer Speedway, all these tracks were half-mile county fair horse tracks. It is probable that most of the Nebraska roadster racing was under dusty and unpleasant conditions.

Poor racing conditions or not the NHRRA developed some good cars and good drivers. After about 1950 a few California built hot rods found their way to Nebraska and these cars ran well. Nebraska racers not only copied these cars but also came up with some ideas of their own. Most of the cars ran well-modified Ford or Mercury V8s but there were some good GMC engines as well as other makes. Nebraska was IMCA (sprint car) territory for many years and some of the Ranger aircraft engines used in these cars found their way into the roadsters.

This is Gordy Shuck's first track roadster. Shuck, in the "helmet" is shown with mechanic Donald Gunn. (Shuck was a winner in the roadsters, sprint cars and stock cars. (Gordy Shuck Collection)

Gordy Shuck was the Nebraska Hot Rod Racing Association champion in 1949 and 1950. In 1951 Andy Anderson moved into the #69 "Belle of Belleville" Mercury V8 roadster and proceeded to just about dominate Nebraska racing for the next two years. "Belle" was built and owned by the Goodrich

Andy Anderson and the "Belle of Belleville" were hard to beat in Nebraska roadster racing. Anderson won two roadster championships, starred in the IMCA sprint cars and is still active as an official at Indianapolis. (Anderson Collection)

This crew kept the "Belle of Belleville" running fast. From left to right Fred Goodrich, Marvin Strong, Paul Folker, Joe Clark, Bob Goodrich, Andy Anderson, Ray Goodrich. The Goodrich brothers owned the car and Anderson did most of the driving. (Frank Brennfoerder Collection)

Andy Anderson apparently won all these trophies on one day at Hastings. This is 1952. (Lorene Goodrich Collection)

Bob Rager wrecked this Ranger powered car at Hastings. The 450 cubic inch Ranger aircraft engine and that rear end no doubt came out of a sprint car (Frank Brennfoerder Collection)

Floyd Adams is pictured with his V8 powered roadster. This is 1950 and Chuck Sears usually did the driving. (Frank Brennfoerder Collection)

Red Melvin works on the Frank Brennfoerder ride someplace in Nebraska. Note that the heat riser on the V8 has been turned into an exhaust port. (Frank Brennfoerder Collection)

brothers in Belleville, Kansas. (Later, this car, with a sprint car body and Anderson at the wheel would be competitive in the Offy rich IMCA.) Some of the other winning Nebraska drivers included Chuck Sears, Gaylord Heiger, Frank Brennfoerder, Jim Gessford and Curly Wadsworth.

By 1953, roadster racing was in bad shape in Nebraska, the car counts were down and the stock cars were booming. The Nebraska Hot Rod Racing Association pretty well evolved into the United Motor Contest Association. This was a sprint car group but roadsters were allowed to run until 1956.

ORD STILL A BIT OF A MYSTERY

There was a sidebar in *Roaring Roadsters* about the roadster races at Ord on July 4 and 5, 1948. Most of this was based on clippings from the *Ord Quiz*. The reporter for the newspaper wrote a very negative report about the races on the first day. The crowd was apparently not pleased and there were quotes like "You can see more speed on the highways these days." Not surprisingly the crowd numbered only 830 on the second day but the *Ord Quiz* admitted the races were better.

Why no speed on the first day? Cars from both Colorado and Nebraska took part in the races. The cars were fast and the drivers experienced. It was unlikely the drivers were intimidated by Ord's high banks. The lack of speed remained pretty much a mystery until I talked to Jim Gessford at the Belleville, Kansas vintage races in 1996. (Jim remembered the Ord races and took part in them.) (He had a ready explanation, "Hell, it was so dusty we couldn't see!" Why didn't the *Ord Quiz* say so?

Another question raised in the *Roaring Roadsters* sidebar was the fact that everybody I contacted in Ord remembered that "there were two California cars at the races." No identification of the California cars ever turned up—I figured that maybe it was a case of mistaken identity of a couple of nice looking Colorado cars.

As we talked at Belleville, Jim Gessford pondered a second and then said, "You know, there were a couple of California cars at that race." Who on earth were they?

The crowd at Ord for the "slow" roadster races on July 4, 1948 was probably like the turnout for this big car race in 1937. (Bill Wood Collection)

The high banks of Ord are evident in this 1936 photo as Jimmy Woods slides by a wrecked car. The roadsters should have gone very fast on this track. (Bill Wood Collection)

Jim Gessford's '27 T-Merc was an exceptionally neat Nebraska car. Gessford shortened the body for a better fit to the 86 inch wheelbase. (Gessford Collection)

Jim Gessford in action at Holdrege. Wire fences were a common hazard at many county fair tracks in the good (?) ole days. (Gessford Collection)

Local farmers look over the Jim Gessford Merc at a race someplace in Nebraska. That's Gessford at the left. (Gessford Collection)

Don Biltoft drove this A-V8. Looks like the body has been shortened. (Frank Brennfoerder Collection)

The Jim Gessford Merc had all the normal goodies. The engine was "3/8s by 3/8s" and used alcohol fuel. (Gessford Collection)

Bob Rager gets a kiss and a trophy for winning the dash at Nelson in 1950. Rager's son Roger raced at Indy in the 1980s. (Frank Brennfoerder Collection)

New Mexico

As in so many states, the prewar roadster racing history of New Mexico is mostly missing. Texas roadster racers ran at a few half-mile horse tracks in the eastern part of the state in the early 1930s. No doubt, local cars and drivers joined them. There was one race held on a dry lake near Clovis. While one report indicates a "high banked" track was built around the shoreline of the lakebed it is possible that the roadsters ran on the lake and maybe it was just straight-away time trials. At this point, nobody knows for sure and research turned up nothing.

Pappy Noe is shown in a c1948 car with his collection of trophies. Noe was over 50 at the time and still winning races. His son Bob is at the left. (Bob Noe Collection)

After the war roadster racing began in the southeastern part of the state with the formation of the Pecos Valley Racing Association and the South West Racing Association (SWRA). From 1947 until 1951, the SWRA sanctioned races at Hobbs, Clovis, Artesia and Carlsbad. The group had a rule that specifically banned sprint cars but this was ignored when the car count was low—which was most of the time. Nobody bothered to crown a SWRA champion but if they had it would have been Earl Emmons. Other top drivers were Paul Pearson, Elton Green and A.M. Farris who come from Texas to race. Of note is that future Indy car great Jud Larson raced a few times with the SWRA. The South Western Auto Racing Association (sometimes called "Club") slowly became a sprint car group with roadsters banned after 1952.

At roughly the same time the SWRA was active there was racing 300 miles away in Gallup. With only five roadsters in town, no organization was formed and help was required from Holbrook, Arizona and Pueblo, Colorado cars. In Gallup it was veteran driver Pappy Noe who took home most of the money. Noe, who was a legend in prewar racing, put a narrowed and shortened Model A body on his sprint car to create a very fast roadster. Like the SWRA the Gallup racers were short of cars so some, were really stripped jalopies while others were forms of sprint cars.

Even though the New Mexico roadsters were pretty much finished by 1953 there was a series of at least ten races held at Aztec, Farmington and Gallup. Most of the races were over holiday weekends with races scheduled for two days. Most of the cars were probably from Arizona—Jay Abney of Phoenix won the majority of the races in Lars Dahlgren's roadster.

An unidentified driver is shown at Aztec in about 1953. This looks like an Arizona or California car. (Joe Winkler Collection)

C.B. Carlson of Carlsbad owned this car. Gordon Woolley drove it at Carlsbad, Roswell, Artesia and Hobbs.

Pappy Noe chopped up a Model A body and put it on his sprint car. The car has a Miller-Schofield OHV head on a Model B Ford block. (Bob Noe Collection)

There should have been roadster racing in Albuquerque with an Unser or two involved but, so far as is known, there was not. Bobby Unser started racing there in 1949 but that was in the coupes.

This photo, from a 1947 Hobbs program, shows Duffy Frauendorfer leading Texan A.M. Ferris. (Dixie Emmons Collection)

Action at Gallup in 1948. That is Charlie Montgomery on the pole in his aptly named "Box Car." The Arizona car, with a Chrysler Six was a lot faster than it looked. (Bob Noe Collection)

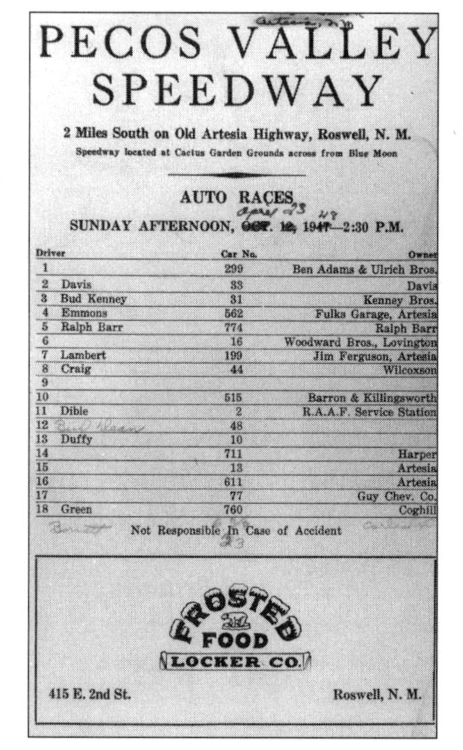

PECOS VALLEY SPEEDWAY

2 Miles South on Old Artesia Highway, Roswell, N. M.

Speedway located at Cactus Garden Grounds across from Blue Moon

AUTO RACES

SUNDAY AFTERNOON, OCT. 12, 1947—2:30 P.M.

Driver	Car No.	Owner
1	299	Ben Adams & Ulrich Bros.
2 Davis	33	Davis
3 Bud Kenney	31	Kenney Bros.
4 Emmons	562	Fulks Garage, Artesia
5 Ralph Barr	774	Ralph Barr
6	16	Woodward Bros., Lovington
7 Lambert	199	Jim Ferguson, Artesia
8 Craig	44	Wilcoxson
9		
10	515	Barron & Killingsworth
11 Dible	2	R.A.A.F. Service Station
12	48	
13 Duffy	10	
14	711	Harper
15	13	Artesia
16	611	Artesia
17	77	Guy Chev. Co.
18 Green	760	Coghill

Not Responsible In Case of Accident

A 1948 program from Roswell. The billing is just for "Auto Races"—no doubt a mixture of roadsters and sprint cars. (Dixie Emmons Collection)

New York

It appears that most of the prewar roadster racing in New York was with cars closer to jalopies on semi-off road courses. There is no doubt most of the cars were roadsters and that engine modifications were permitted. In the western part of the state, near Batavia, there was a track called "Satan's Playground"—future stock car and Indy driver, Al Keller, got his start there. In Rochester, there is evidence that there was oval track roadster racing. Further east, in the Albany area, several jalopy tracks operated. Ida Mae Speedway at Schodack was an off road track with a creek to ford. McKown's Grove at Guilderland and Red Finn's Track at Claverack were both ovals so the cars must have been closer to true track roadsters despite the jalopy name.

It is hard to give a name to this car but it ran with the roadsters at Penney Royal Speedway in Leon. (Lou Ensworth Collection)

After the war the Rochester Roadster Racing Association (RRRA) was formed in the western part of New York. This group sanctioned races at a half dozen tracks although most were at the Hemlock Fairgrounds. During that time there was a fine midget track at the Buffalo Municipal Stadium but the RRRA ran only one exhibition race at this speedway. The top RRRA drivers were Jerry Earl, Bill Chick, Irv Morrison and Danny Daniels.

About 150 miles southwest of Rochester there was roadster racing in the tiny town of Leon at Penney Royal Speedway. While the name seems auspicious, this was a rough oval in a cow pasture. Racing started with primitive roadsters but some of these evolved into nice track hot rods. Penney Royal also developed some very good drivers. Among these were Lloyd Moore, Bud Fanelle, Mike Egan and Carl Pintegro. The 1950 NASCAR Grand National Champion, Bill Rexford, began his career in a very poor car at Penney Royal. Thanks to Jamestown car dealer, Julian Buesink, both Rexford and Lloyd Moore were able to move into NASCAR late model stock car racing.

In the remainder of New York, it seems that roadster racing was rather disorganized. Extensive research has turned up some bits and pieces. There was racing from about 1949 to 1951 at perhaps 20 tracks in Central and Eastern New York. Most of it was with local cars and drivers although some of the better drivers traveled to other tracks. If any roadster group was formed anywhere in this rather large area it has been forgotten.

In the Albany area, in Eastern New York, there

was weekly racing at the Pine Bowl in Troy, at Westerlo and Athens. Bob Hart of East Nassau, New York, remembers that most of the cars used Model A or early V8 bodies. Hart was one of the better drivers as was Bob Whitbeck who was sometimes billed as the "New York State Roadster Champion." Whitbeck regularly made trips to run with the Eastern Racing Association in Virginia. Some of the other Albany area drivers were Jim Bedell, Jim Cox, Howie Westervelt and Jerry Niver. Most of the roadster races paid about $50 to win—it appears that the group was short of cars.

North of Albany, in the Glens Falls area, there were a number of roadsters that ran on local tracks. Thanks to historian and photographer, Les King of Watervliet, New York, some information is available. There was racing at Adirondack Speedway in West Glens Falls, at McGregor Speedway in Wilton, Schuylerville Speedway and further north at Ticonderoga and Warrensburg as well as at other tracks. In all of these races the roadsters ran with the stock cars. The roadsters were mostly '33 or '34 Fords but there were some A-V8s running. It is probable that stock, or stock appearing, engines

Jerry Earl in action at the Hemlock Fairgrounds. Some of the obvious hazards shown here were later removed. (Bob Chaddock Collection-Len Campagno Photo)

were required. A few Chevy Sixes ran but there were no four cylinder Model A or B Ford conversions. The roadsters were required to have cage rollbars but, even so, running against full-bodied stockers sounds a bit hazardous. The insurance companies agreed and this, along with a shortage of

Bill Chick was one of the better Rochester Roadster Racing Association drivers. He is shown in the Bob Chaddock Plymouth-Model A. (Bob Chaddock Collection-Lou Campagno Photo)

roadster bodies, ended roadster racing by about 1951. Some of the better Eastern New York drivers were Wally LaBelle, Hollis Hammond, Bob Shardone and Art Pratt. Pratt later moved to Southern California and starred in the sprints and modifieds.

Bob Whitbeck at Williams Grove, Pennsylvania. Whitbeck won a lot of New York roadster races and was billed as the "New York State Roadster Champion." (Carl Sweigart Collection)

Bob Hart was a winner in the New York roadsters. He is shown here at Williams Grove in 1949. (Hart Collection—Frank Smith Photo)

In 1949, John Carpenter started a Hartford, Connecticut based group called the "American Hot Rod Racing Club." There were lavish plans to race roadsters, modified stocks and coupes at well-known New England and New York tracks. Most of this apparently never happened. Bob Hart ran with this group and recalls they held a combination midget, stock car and roadster show at the New York Fairgrounds in Altamont. (The same type of program was held at Avon, Connecticut and West Springfield, Massachusetts.)

There is almost certainly some New York roadster racing information that is still missing. There should have been roadster racing in the Syracuse area—extensive research has turned up nothing. It is also possible that there was a roadster group in Buffalo.

Thanks to Bob Hart, Les King and Jess Cunningham for help with roadster racing in Central and Eastern New York.

Bob Hart in action at Burden Lake Speedway in 1950. Hart is driving the Cliff Wright Ford Six—not too many of these engines ran in the east. (Pat Hart Photo)

A wrecked car sits on the guardrail at the Ticonderoga Fairgrounds. "Roadsters" like this ran with full bodied stock cars. (Les King Photo)

A couple of roadsters get tangled up at Burden Lake as a coupe slides around the outside. (Pat Hart Photo)

Al Moses Sr. drove one of the biggest roadsters ever to race. This Cadillac V8 looks like about a 1934 Model. Moses eventually flipped the Caddie. (Les King Photo)

Floyd Battise takes a victory lap after win at Adirondack Speedway in West Glens Falls. Looks like a rough and rocky track. (Les King Photo)

Pete Corey was one of the greats in New York stock car racing. He took a few roadster rides and chalked up this win at Perth in Bob Whitbeck's #7. (Pete Corey Collection)

Bob Shardone is shown after a feature win at Adirondack Speedway. There was roadster racing at this West Glens Falls oval for several years. (Les King Photo)

George Tubbs in the coupe and Roy Ball in the roadster battle for position. The roadsters won most of the races in these mixed West Glens Falls events. (Les King Photo)

Red Sprague is towed in after a crash at Adirondack Speedway. (Les King Photo)

A CASE OF MISIDENTIFICATION

Left–Bob Badgley is shown in his cutdown coupe "Lucky 7" at Penney Royal Speedway in 1948 (Lou Ensworth Collection)

Bob Badgley flips at Penney Royal. That less than sturdy rollbar is flexing but it wound up doing the job. (Carol Badgley Collection—Jim Curtis Photo)

Bob Badgley, with only minor injuries, is helped from his overturned car. Badgley soon switched, perhaps wisely, to the stock cars. (Carol Badgley Collection—Donald Curtis Photo)

Unfortunately, photo captions in racing books all too often misidentify drivers and other people. There were plenty of these in *Roaring Roadsters* and I am sure despite the best efforts of all involved there are similar errors in this book.

One of the most serious errors in photo identification in *Roaring Roadsters* was in the New York chapter. The driver of car "Lucky 7" at Penney Royal Speedway was identified as George Ott and it was noted that Ott had been killed in this car. The error went undetected until Carol Badgley of Greenhurst, New York saw the photo in the book. The driver was her husband, Bob Badgley, who did indeed crash "Lucky 7" at Penney Royal. Badgley not only survived the crash but passed away only a few years ago. Carol was kind enough to supply the photos of her husband's adventure at Penney Royal.

Right–Art Pratt is shown at Corinth. Pratt, later a star in Southern California sprints and modifieds, is driving a '29 Chrysler with a Ford V8 engine. (Les King Photo)

Left–Bob Hart is pushed out for what was almost certainly the only roadster race ever held in Connecticut. This is Avon in 1949. (Pat Hart Photo)

Cars line up for a 1950 race at the Ticonderoga Fairgrounds. Vernon Beach is in #23 but the roadster driver is unknown—his A-V8 would soon be required to have a cage rollbar. (Les King Photo)

A primitive and battered machine but none the less a roadster. Roy Ball is the driver and he has just chalked up a win at Adirondack Speedway. (Les King Photo)

George Dalbey won races at Adirondack. He's pictured with mechanic Conrad Mueller. (Les King Photo)

Wally LaBelle was one of the big winners at Adirondack Speedway. While the roadsters had cage rollbars helmet regulations must have been a bit lax. (Les King Photo)

Ray Therriene was years ahead of his time in chassis design—strictly 1997 space frame engineering. At one point Therriene used a length of chain as a seat belt! (Les King Photo)

Jack Beena churns up the dust at Adirondack Speedway in 1951. (Les King Photo)

N. Dakota

Harley Gunkel in #762 and Red Stark tangle in the dust at Bismarck. Gunkel won some races in his V8—Stark is running a Fronty Model T Ford engine. (Gunkel Collection)

There wasn't much roadster racing in North Dakota. No evidence of prewar racing has been found but, knowing the way things were, it is very possible that roadsters of some kind raced in the state in the 1930s.

The Valley Roadster Club was formed in the Fargo-Moorhead (Minnesota) area in 1949. Street hot rods were rare in North Dakota so the group pretty well started with nothing and had to construct cars. Most of the cars were A-V8s with a sprinkling of Model As, Model Bs and even a Fronty T. The first roadster race in the Fargo area was in July of 1949 at Ada in adjacent Minnesota.

During the remainder of 1949, the Valley Roadster Club ran races at Detroit Lakes in Minnesota and at Fargo, Bismarck, Forman and Aneta in North Dakota. Some of the races were under the promotion of Bruce Byers and his "Thrills Inc." while local service clubs sponsored other races. Purses can only be described as "small" and the big money that some had anticipated never happened. There were ongoing problems with dust—the racers complained, the fans complained and so did anybody who lived within a mile of the racetracks.

Probably in 1950 the Valley Roadster Club, along with Thrills Inc. built a racetrack at Glyndon, Minnesota—a few miles east of Fargo. The track turned out to be poorly designed with long straightaways and sharp turns that the roadsters just could not negotiate. The hot rods never raced there.

The death of popular Orville Johnson at Aneta in the fall of 1950 apparently helped seal the fate of roadster racing in North Dakota. No formal announcement was made but racing simply did not resume in 1951.

Right–A lineup at Fargo in 1950. Orville Johnson is on the pole in his Model A and Bruce Byers is in the cutdown '38 Ford convertible on the outside. (Dell Byers Collection)

North Dakota Hot Rods

Left: Orey Hansen

Right: Jerome Verlinden Alice, N.D.

Left: Speed Malstrom Fargo, N.D.

Left: Eugene Landstrom

Right: Don Anderson Enderlin, N.D.

Left: Sylvester Dimm Alice, N.D.

Below: Red Volk

Out of my way; I'm in a hurry!

Wonder who will cross the finish line first?

Page 14

RACING WHEE

As indicated in the photos most of the North Dakota cars were fairly nice looking track roadsters. One photo shows the dust that was a persistent problem. (From Racing Wheels—Russ Daley Collection)

Northern California

To an extent, roadster racing began on a big time speedway. This was in 1931 and the Oakland Mile was being built for AAA National Championship racing. This high-banked oval, constructed for the then astronomical cost of $100,000, would be one of the finest tracks in the United States. A program of roadster races took place a few weeks before the speedway officially opened. The high banks had not yet been constructed but the straightaways were in place. The cars cut across the dirt infield to form a roughly square course. It was definitely not a high-class event and it is very possible that the roadster racers were trespassing. It is known that the promoter ran off with the money and that future midget and Indy great, Fred Agabashian, was a competitor at age seventeen.

In the early and mid-1930s most of the roadster racing was on the banked five-eighths mile track at San Jose. There was no actual roadster organization formed but a variety of promoters put on moderately successful races at San Jose. At one point, a guaranteed purse of $250 was offered with $75 to win the main—good money in those depression years. Most of the drivers competing in these races would go on to become top competitors in northern California for the next couple of decades. Duane Carter and Fred Agabashian went on to national fame although Agabashian's career suffered when he was seriously injured at San Jose in 1934.

The first roadster organization in northern California came with the forming of the Bay Cities Roadster Racing Association (BCRRA) in 1939. This group raced on a flat half-mile track at Oakland Speedway, at San Jose, Calistoga and

San Jose in 1934 and Fred Agabashian has just won a race in this Chevy roadster. (Bob Garner Collection)

A group of roadster drivers at San Jose in 1934. Standing is Duke Foley, Sitting (L to R) George Ruckatani, Bonstell and Al Chasteen. Ruckatani later owned sprint cars in the Midwest. (Chick Lastiri Collection)

This advertisement in Coast Auto Racing helped attract good roadster fields to San Jose in 1934. (Bob Garner Collection)

Oakland in 1936. This is probably a big car race during a period when there was a shortage of cars. Note that the #4 roadster has a makeshift tail. Car #5, probably Buck Whitmer, was normally run as a modified with no tail. (Dick Downes Collection)

San Jose in about 1938 and this might be Eddie Bosio. (Dick Downes Collection)

Mauri King won the 1939 Bay Cities Roadster Racing Association championship. (Buck Bowers Collection)

other cities. For the first time point standings were kept and Mauri King was crowned champion. In 1940 and 1941 Buck Bowers won the title. Both drove very fast four cylinder Chevies with the Oldsmobile three-port head and other goodies—Clem Sala owned both cars. Purses during this time were reported as "not much."

World War II halted all racing in 1942. In 1943, an event took place that doubtless effected northern California roadster racing. The BCRRA members had become more interested in the midgets and voted to drop "Roadster " from the group's name. The result was that when WW II was over late in 1945 there was no existing roadster organization and racing with these cars was slow to get underway. A year of what would have been a time of some very lucrative purses was wasted. (This was true of the roadsters all over the United States—only Mutual in Indiana had a roadster organization ready to race.)

Post war racing started with street roadsters at Oakland Stadium—a different track than the Oakland Mile, which had been torn down during the war. The cars—soon called hot rods—immediately caught on with the fans. In short order the Northern California Roadster Racing Association was formed. By 1947, there was racing five to six nights a week at various San Francisco Bay Area tracks—the street rods quickly became track roadsters. Crowds were good and so were the purses—$1500 was commonplace. As racers will do (and STILL DO!) squabbles developed so in 1948 another group, the Racing Roadsters Incorporated (RRI), was formed. Both the RRI and the NCRRA kept busy in 1948 but purses probably averaged no more than $750. In 1949, there was less roadster racing as the stock cars were taking over with their fender bending action. A bit later, the RRI and the NCRRA combined to form the United Roadster Association (URA) and racing went on intermittently until about 1953.

Like with the earlier roadsters the post war hot rods trained some excellent race drivers. On a local level midget and sprint car, drivers rosters clear up into the 1960s were filled with roadster graduates. Drivers who made it to Indy were Ed Elisian, Elmer George, Wayne Selzer, 1955 winner Bob SweiKert and Bob Veith. Earl Motter and Dickie Reese also drove roadsters a few times.

During the roadster era there was racing at several "outlaw" tracks and additional roadster groups were formed in the Watsonville area and at Sacramento. In Watsonville, the Central California Roadster Association sanctioned races at Palm Beach Speedway in 1947 and 1948. Paul Kamm was the 1947 champion and drivers like Bill Peters, Johnny Lomanto and Johnny Key were also winners.

At Sacramento, the Capital Racing Association sanctioned roadster races at Lazy J Speedway. Racing started in 1946 and continued through 1948. For a time in 1947, there were races twice a week. At first, Lazy J was dirt and the dust was terrible. Later on it was paved and became a nice little semi-banked oval. Drivers who did well at Lazy J included Paul Kamm and Wayne Selzer. Late in 1948, the NCRRA raced at Lazy J but crowds were down by then. I ran there and had a good night but the payoff was only $13.95. Unfortunately, no photos of Lazy J racing could be found. As of a few years ago, the track was still visible from the freeway east of Sacramento.

A nice looking San Jose roadster but no identification on the driver. (Dick Downes Collection)

A quartet of BCRRA racers in about 1940. From left to right, Chick Lastiri, Gene Figone, Norm Holtkamp and Pat Ciramelli. (Chick Lastiri Collection)

Buck Bowers, on the left and Mauri King both won BCRRA championships in these well-built Clem Sala Chevies. (Buck Bowers Collection)

Gene Figone in action at San Jose. Figone was well on his way to racing stardom when he was killed in a roadster at Santa Rosa in 1941. (Dick Downes Collection)

Johnny Soares, at the left and Norm Holtkamp smile after a 1938 Oakland roadster race. Both went on to be winning midget drivers and Soares is still promoting races in northern California. (Buck Bowers Collection)

Johnny Soares takes a nasty spill on the Oakland half-mile track in about 1940. Soares wore no seat belt and was saved from serious injury when his foot got caught between the clutch and brake pedals. (Chalmers-Davies Collection)

Buck Bowers leads an unidentified driver on the flat half miler at Oakland. The high bank of the Oakland Mile is visible in the background. (Dick Downes Collection)

It is hard to believe but Rod Harrison was only slightly injured in this 1941 Calistoga crash. (Buck Bowers Collection)

Chick Lastiri knocked down two fences at Calistoga when a right front hub broke. Lastiri later fielded some very good sprint cars in West Coast competition. (Chick Lastiri Collection)

Gabby Gilbert at Oakland in 1938. Gilbert usually smoked a cigar while racing. His real first name is unknown. (Dick Downes Collection)

An unknown driver gets ready to be pushed off at San Jose. Looks like a four banger. (Al Slinker Collection)

Al Slinker's first racecar. He taped up the numbers and drove it to classes at the University of California. (Al Slinker Collection)

Tony Cancilla's A-V8 at San Jose. What on earth is a V8 Hisso"? (Al Slinker Collection)

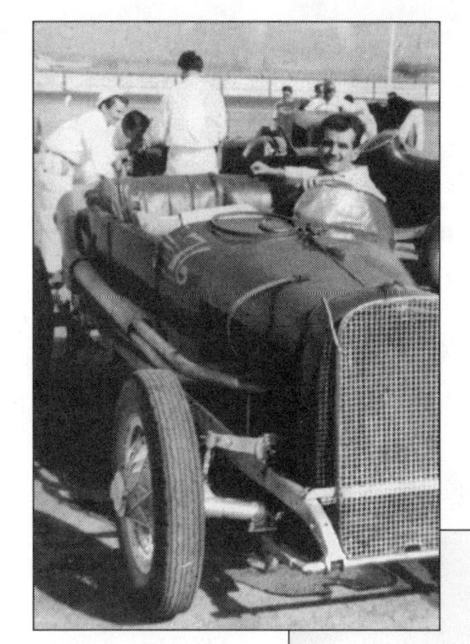

A prewar roadster at San Jose in late 1946. It was not competitive against the V8s. (Al Slinker Collection)

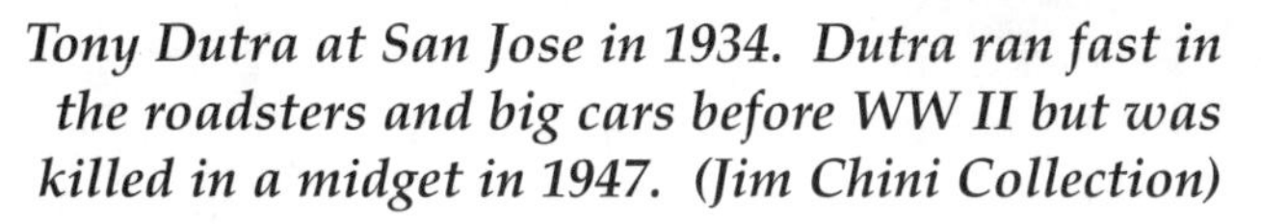

Tony Dutra at San Jose in 1934. Dutra ran fast in the roadsters and big cars before WW II but was killed in a midget in 1947. (Jim Chini Collection)

George Mehalas in his very nice looking street rod at Oakland. Mehalas did well in the roadsters and later starred in the sprints. (Vern Hart Collection)

Car owner Ben Hubbard in 1947. Hubbard was one of the first to build a real track roadster in northern California. He was a long time supporter of auto racing. (Rod Eschenburg Collection)

Sam Hawks chases Andy Botto at Pacheco (aka Contra Costa Stadium. Both the hot rods and the midgets knocked down those wooden fences regularly. (Bruce Craig Collection)

This is probably the first roadster race at Oakland. Among drivers who can be identified are Eddie Bosio in #101 and Al Slinker on the inside of the second row. (Don Radbruch Photo-Jim Chini Collection)

Bob SweiKert in 1947. The 1955 Indy champion was a winner in the roadsters from the beginning but not too popular with his fellow drivers. (Bruce Craig Collection)

Pacheco and that's Tommy Cheek in #55 and Manual Sanchez in #1. (Dick Liebfritz Collection)

Left–Pat Patrick in one of the two Hubbard Auto Parts cars. Patrick drove in only a few races. (Tom Motter Collection)

Right– Les Cash on the San Jose dirt track in 1948. Cash ran a four banger against the big V8s with some success. He now lives in Nevada and is still building four bangers. (Sowle Collection)

This is almost certainly Andy Botto at Pacheco in 1947. It took a patient man to do all the masking for the paint job on the Chevy Six. (Bruce Craig Collection)

Sam Hawks in action at Pacheco in the Ben Hubbard Merc. Hawks almost certainly raced before World War II but where and what? (Bruce Craig Collection)

Joe Valente kicks up some clay at Pacheco. The car runs two front springs—unusual. (Bruce Craig Collection)

Butler Ruggard at Stockton in 1948. He began his career at Lazy J Speedway in Sacramento. (Walt James Collection)

Johnny Key at Oakland. Car owner Jay D. Rowe also owned Salinas Speedway and was a longtime Key sponsor. (Rod Eschenburg Collection)

Chet Richards has a dirty face after an Oakland win in the McFadden Ford Six. This race was on the high-banked five-eighths mile track. (Tom Motter Collection)

This is a constructor's shop in San Jose—just like NASCAR isn't it? Clyde Palmer (center) is building his roadster in the backyard. (Clyde Palmer Collection)

Joe Valente at Pacheco. The Merc sits high in the chassis but Valente made it work, as did Wayne Selzer later on. (Rod Eschenburg Collection)

George Mehalas gets a trophy from pretty Mary Zable. Her husband, Bill, was chief timer for the NCRRA. (Valcon Photo—Bob Veith Collection)

Walt James came up to Oakland to race on occasion. That "whitewall" tire indicates he has scraped the concrete wall. James is currently very active in vintage racing. (Rod Eschenburg Collection)

Ed Elisian in a hurry at Modesto. Controversy and criticism marked the latter part of Elisian's career but he was a fine race driver. (Bruce Craig Collection)

Action on the 60 degree banked turn at Oakland. These cars are running a bit too low—the really fast way around was about three feet further up the track. Cars often bounced off the concrete wall. (Rod Eschenburg Collection)

Jimmy Davies drove Walt James' Ford Six at Oakland. Davies drove at Indy and was a big winner in AAA midgets before being killed in one of the small cars. (Bill Chubbuck Collection)

Left–This is probably the same Clyde Palmer car. A bodyman by trade Palmer has molded in the front of the T body. (Clyde Palmer Collection)

THE STORY OF #62

Most track roadsters had very short lives. They would get wrecked and be salvaged for parts or rebuilt with changed bodies, engines and even frames. Number 62, in pretty much the original form, was around for about ten years.

The car was built by BCRRA president Ken Van Woert in about 1938. The prewar history is a bit muddled but Buck Bowers remembers driving the car at Oakland and destroying an OHV T engine that Van Woert had spent a year building. Van Woert probably drove the car too, but at San Jose on August 6, 1938, it is almost certain that George Ameral drove the car. Ameral won the main that day and this was the first roadster race that I ever saw.

At some point before World War II Curly Wells bought the car and installed a Four-Port Riley engine. After the war Chuck Harwood acquired the car and ran it regularly in NCRRA events. Harwood probably ran the Riley but some photos show a flathead in the car so maybe he had a spare four banger. At any rate, midway in 1948 Harwood blew the engine and the car was side-lined. Enter yours truly on the scene. I had a fairly good Merc engine in my heavy, outdated tank-like #74. Why not put the good engine in Harwood's lightweight #62? It took a lot of cutting and chopping to put the Merc in the space occupied by the four cylinder engine but, in a week or so, this was done. Harwood and I took turns driving with moderate success. Then came Modesto on October 17, 1948. The photos illustrate the sad demise of #62. I must have said something like, "Oops, sorry!" My engine was removed and the remains given back to Chuck Harwood.

Until only a year ago I did not realize I had destroyed such a historic roadster—one that I had seen win a race ten years earlier.

This is #62 at San Jose in 1946. The car looked like this when it was raced in 1938 to 1941. (Al Slinker Collection)

Don Radbruch flips #62 at Modesto. A lot of help was provided by Herb Hill. (Nancy Radbruch Collection)

Chuck Harwood slides through a turn at Pacheco in 1947—the car was #6 at this point. (Ray Hiatt Collection)

The end of #62. The driver? It hurt! (Les Radbruch Photo)

A pitman looks up at the 60-degree bank at Oakland. The track was spectacular and fast but, obviously, had only a one car groove. (Gordy Sutherland Collection)

Clyde Palmer in the Masterini Ford Six at San Jose. Palmer went fast in this car—and faster in the San Jose modifieds ten to twenty years later. (Clyde Palmer Collection)

Author Don Radbruch knocks down some fence on the one-mile Stockton Fairgrounds track in 1951. California roadsters did not run these dangerous horse tracks too often. (Nancy Radbruch Collection)

Oregon's Len Sutton visited at Stockton late in 1948. The talented future Indy driver virtually dominated Pacific Northwest roadster racing and probably did OK at Stockton. (Jim Abreu Photo—Dick Jones Collection)

Don Radbruch left the Paul Kamm Merc in this rather precarious position at Stockton. Splintering fences on this day in 1951 painfully injured two drivers. (Nancy Radbruch Collection)

Les Radbruch found the crash wall at San Jose to be very stout. Car #69 was a well-built roadster with a tube frame but did not handle well. (Diane Radbruch Collection)

Elmer George at Oakland in 1949. George's son Tony now runs Indianapolis Speedway and the IRL.

George Mehalas is in #5 at San Jose. This beautiful roadster was featured on the cover of Hot Rod Magazine in 1949. (Dennis Arnold Photo)

Les Radbruch in 1950—looks like he has been doing some dirty work on the car. Radbruch did OK in the roadsters and moved on to the sprint cars. (Bob Barkhimer Photo)

This is Al Gaetano who came back from serious injuries in 1947 to become a top ranked hot rod pilot. (Sowle Collection)

Les Radbruch in the Frank Smith Merc. This was the first car built by Chuck Tatum who is still building racecars. Tatum builds Formula Vee sports cars. (Diane Radbruch Collection)

WHAT IS IT?

Andy McNair owned and drove this unusual roadster at San Jose and other California tracks in 1934. In an attempt to identify the car, these photos were sent to "experts" all over the country. The photos have also appeared in several "old timers" publications. The best guesses are a Whippet and a Falcon Knight. McNair has made changes on the car and those appear to be Model A wheels. Perhaps there is even a hopped up Model A engine. A puzzle to ponder.

Andy McNair is shown in his roadster in about 1934. Note the "boat tail" on the car and the two exhaust pipes that are coming from the right side of the engine. (Art Bagnall Collection)

It looks like McNair has grafted Model A front and rear axles on to whatever the car is. McNair later drove midgets in the San Francisco area. (Art Bagnall Collection)

Things get a bit crowded at the start of a Devils Bowl race in Salinas. Spectator protection is minimal. (Lomanto Collection)

Johnny Lomanto leads Norm Garland in #23. These Devils Bowl cars were really more jalopy than track roadster but they were fast. (Lomanto Collection)

Johnny Lomanto is surrounded by an admiring crowd after a Devils Bowl win in 1946. That's John Alemand in the cloth helmet—he later built Alemand Speedway. (Lomanto Collection)

Actually all roadster racers were outlaws. "Outlaw" in the 1940s or '50s meant any racing group outside of the high and mighty American Automobile Association—the AAA or "Three A". The AAA controlled Indy and most of the major tracks in the US—everything else was outlaw. In roadster terminology outlaw meant racing not sanctioned by an organized group. Rules might be looser, payoffs sometimes questionable and, all too often, no insurance for the drivers. Outlaw roadster racing was even more dangerous than organized racing.

Life was simpler in those days. Just build a racetrack, scare up some cars and go racing. Such was the way things started in 1946 at Devils Bowl in Salinas. Paul Kamm remembers it this way. "I heard there were going to be races so I jumped in my Chevy Four roadster and went out to watch. Kamm was immediately recruited to race—he and three other "track roadsters" that showed up. Somehow the four cars managed to put on a crowd pleasing show as Kamm won what passed for a main event and took home $100.

Future races at Devils Bowl attracted somewhat better fields but there were seldom more than ten cars on hand. The track, variously reported as being from one to three eighths of a mile, was a bit up and down but was an oval. Johnny Lomanto was by far the dominant driver in a cutdown GMC that probably started life as a pickup. Safety regulations at Devils Bowl were nil and most drivers didn't even wear helmets but, so far as is known, there were no serious injuries. The track operated only for a short time and must have closed around the time Alemand Speedway opened some 30 miles to the north.

John Alemand had raced at Devils Bowl and perhaps this inspired him to build a racetrack on his ranch near Gilroy. He drained a stock watering pond and created a rather lopsided oval that ran successful races for the better part of three seasons. Alemand was a spectacular place. One straightaway was downhill where the cars would hit near 90 mph and then scrub off speed by sliding sideways around a wide banked turn. Most of the Alemand cars were crude but, on occasion, some nice looking street rods would show up to race.

Alemand car #44 has a four cylinder Chevy with the Olds three port head. This car probably raced before World War II. (Vern McCarthy Collection)

Purses at Alemand were as high as $1100—comparable to most of the "legitimate" tracks in the area. Johnny Lomanto was back with an improved version of his Devils Bowl GMC and won a lot of races. Paul Kamm and Norm Garland also did OK. All three of these drivers would move on to more organized roadster racing in the region. At Alemand, there were three driver fatalities. The last fatality helped end racing at Alemand but, by that time, probably early 1948, the crowds had dwindled anyway.

Johnny Lomanto became somewhat of a legend at Alemand when he won ten main events at the track in 1947. Word of his winning ways filtered up to the Oakland area and the Northern California Roadster Racing Association sent a car to Alemand to "blow off that guy in the GMC." It didn't work. Lomanto won the main that day for a $300 payoff and then added $50 for soundly trouncing the visitor in a match race.

Oscar Betts in a cutdown something leads an unidentified driver in what is obviously a street rod. Betts later drove some very good track roadsters. (Lomanto Collection)

A couple of cars get the checkered flag at Alemand Speedway in 1947. The track afforded excellent viewing sites for spectators. (Vern Hart Collection)

Action at Alemand with Johnny Lomanto at left. (Vern McCarthy Collection)

Earl Smith in action at Palm Beach Speedway in Watsonville. The half-mile "D" shaped track was a fast and dangerous place. (Vern Hart Collection)

Johnny Lomanto at Palm Beach. Lomanto's GMC had the power that was needed for the often loose track conditions. (Vern Hart Collection)

Author Don Radbruch lines up for one of his first races at Watsonville. At left is Carl White who was killed in #3 a week later. (Nancy Radbruch Collection)

As midget racing died down around 1951 some midget drivers drove roadsters. Dickie Reese was one of them and as his autograph caption indicates it was a one shot deal. (Don Scott Collection)

Midget star Earl Motter in a rare roadster ride at Oakland. Motter, who also drove AAA-USAC Champ cars, was a rough and tough customer so roadster drivers were content that he stayed away. (Tom Motter Collection)

Norm Garland starts a series of flips at Salinas that left him seriously injured. Elmer George is in #86 and Johnny Key in #55. (Dennis Arnold Photo—Ray Hiatt Collection)

A big man? Nope, it is a little roadster. This is a micro-midget at Ukiah in 1959 and owner-driver Dick Thornton has fashioned a roadster body for this car. Thornton's car used a Salisbury Motor Scooter engine. Too bad a Merc wouldn't fit! (Dick Thornton Collection—Bob Buchanan Photo)

FIRST RACE

Buck Bowers was one of the better pre-World War II drivers in northern California. He was the BCRRA champion in 1940 and 1941. Here, written some 58 years later, is Buck's story of his first race.

"As I remember, I started driving in 1938. I believe my first race was at the old five-eighths mile track in San Jose. I don't remember the car or car owner. I do remember thinking I was going at least 150 miles per hour! I guess there were about twelve cars in the race and I came in twentieth. My goggles were shattered; my nose was bleeding. I could hardly see from being hit by pieces of the track surface breaking up. I was sick to my stomach from oil fumes and very tired."

"Why I continued to drive, I will never know!" I suspect that most of us who drove roadsters feel the same way about that first confusing and thrilling (scary?) race. Come on—be honest!

Buck Bowers is shown with car owner Clem Sala in 1940. Sala's four cylinder Chevy roadsters won three BCRRA championships. Mauri King won the title in 1939 and Bowers in 1940-41. (Buck Bowers Collection)

Ohio

While some information on early Ohio roadster racing has been found it appears that most of it is missing. There was roadster racing at Hamilton in 1931 and again in 1937—surely there were races in the intervening years. There is documentation of roadster racing at Sharon Speedway on the Pennsylvania border. Future racing great Mike Klapak won a 100-mile race there in 1932 and reportedly dominated an eleven race series of hundred milers in 1931 and 1932. It would seem that racing like this would have continued up until WW II but, other than a race at Newark in 1941, nothing has been found.

The only other evidence of prewar racing is at the Ramble Inn near Alger. Based on the photos these were very crude cars. Most were Model A roadsters but coupes also ran as well as unidentified touring cars. The Ramble Inn was a roadhouse—fancy name for a bar. The races were most likely held to bring business to the establishment.

It is dusty going at Ramble Inn near Alger in the late 1930s. (Tom Ward Collection)

The Ramble Inn driver is nearly pitched out as his roadster hits a bump. No seat belts—no helmets. (Tom Ward Collection)

This is one of the better-looking Ramble Inn cars. Check that firesuit! (Tom Ward Collection)

A couple of Ramble Inn cars struggle through what might be described as a heavy track. (Tom Ward Collection)

Primitive? Yes, but the very strong Mutual Racing Association started with cars like this. So far as is known the Ramble Inn cars stayed this way. (Tom Ward Collection)

Mike Michael is shown in his A-V8 in 1947. The engine came out of racing boat—hence the unusual headers. Michael raced boats but left the driving to others in the roadsters. (Mike Michael Collection)

Whether or not admission was charged at the races or if the payoffs were in cash or beer is not known.

After WW II Ohio roadster racing got going in the eastern part of the state with the formation of the Ohio Speedway Association, (See the sidebar on the rather unusual details of this group). In western Ohio, it didn't take long for the Mutual Racing Association from neighboring Indiana to schedule races at Dayton, Cincinnati and Columbus.

Another roadster group in Ohio was the Dayton based Triangle Racing Association (TRA). The TRA was formed in 1947 and, during at least part of that year, was the sanctioning body at Dayton Speedway. Dayton was one of the best paying roadster tracks in the state for several years. Battles over a well paying track often lead to all out wars between roadster groups but not so in Dayton. The Mutual Racing Association sanctioned most of this racing and, apparently, Triangle went along with this invasion of their home turf. Research by Dale Fairfax of Indianapolis indicates that both Mutual and Triangle cars and drivers supported the Dayton races as well as events at Shady Bowl near De Graff. It appears that the relationship between the two groups wasn't always perfect. At one point four Mutual hotshots showed up at Shady Bowl and finished one through four in the main event. Triangle found some reason not to pay the Mutual racers—there must have been one heck of an argument! Triangle was probably the sanctioning body for the relatively few races held at New Bremen.

In western Ohio there was another roadster group formed in 1949. This was the Buckeye Roadster Association and they raced almost exclusively in the tiny town of Landeck. This was an example of a small town organization starting with near nothing and turning it into a successful racing operation. The first Buckeye cars were few and they were primitive. The Buckeye racers were quick learners and they had the nearby Mutual Racing Association cars to copy from. The racing at Landeck went on for several years and drew good crowds. The top drivers included Bud Claypool, Don Jones and George Place who built and drove some fast Hudsons.

There was a Northern Ohio Roadster Association and perhaps an Ohio Roadster Association operating in central Ohio. Sadly, it appears that these groups and racers have been forgotten.

This is the Pete Allen car at Dayton in 1947. (Mike Michael Collection)

Walt Schearer at Shady Grove in 1950. This Fred Vickery V8 ran in several Little 500 races at Anderson, Indiana. (Gail Alloway Collection)

Chester Pratt at Shady Bowl. He was a regular in the Southern Indiana Racing Association. (Gail Alloway Collection)

L.T. Meyers at Shady Bowl in 1953. The pitcrew is, left to right, Bob Willaby, Kenny Heilman, John Fry and Don Powell. (Dale Fairfax Collection)

Howard Mowell in the fast Lee Izor GMC at Shady Bowl in September of 1951. Lee Izor is at left and Charles Izor at the right. The body is from a c1916 Saxon. (Gail Alloway Collection)

Right–This is the ex-Joe Walls Hudson now owned by Carl Bratton. No ID on the driver in this 1950 Shady Bowl photo but it looks like Junior Kunz. (Gail Alloway Collection)

Red Amick and Red Renner drove this Bob Fiene Merc. Fiene was from Arlington Heights IL but the car has the look of a California built machine. Shady Bowl in 1954. (Gail Alloway Collection)

Dick Jordan is the driver of the Russ Lowery Ford Six. This is Shady Bowl on September 5, 1950. (Gail Alloway Collection)

Dick Elliott drove his own Ford Six in Triangle Racing Association events. The Model A body has been shortened to better fit on the 86 inch wheelbase chassis. (Gail Alloway Collection)

Elzie Whetnall drove this C.O. Gray V8 at Shady Bowl. (Gail Alloway Collection)

Bob Wilson has a ride in the nice looking Hardesty Chevy. Don Jones usually drove this car at Landeck. (Gail Alloway Collection)

Red Crammer is in the Charles Black V8 at Shady Bowl. This car ran on many tracks in Ohio. (Gail Alloway Collection)

THE OSA AND NASCAR

The Ohio Speedway Association (OSA) began racing in a mostly disorganized fashion in 1946. Jack Bensley promoted races as the Cuyahoga County Fairgrounds in Berea, near Cleveland. The phrase, "run what yuh brung" is overused but appropriate for early OSA races. Here is a sampling of the entry list for an early race—some names may be misspelled

Spike Gilliland............................Model A with V8 engine
Bob James.............'35 Ford coupe less roof and fenders
Art Volpe..'35 Ford Roadster
Steve Lesick......................Model A with Hal conversion
Mike Cindrich or Cliff Coleman..................Model A coupe with a V8
Tony Banick..Hudson roadster
Al Dorus...Model A
John Dorus...'33 Ford Sedan
Elmer Gutzman..Buick Sedan
Chuck Benson..Plymouth Sedan
Dan Odl..Stutz Bearcat
Harold DeWolf..Plymouth Sedan
Tiny Quillan...Model A roadster
Cliff Coryea...Hudson Coupe

Unfortunately, no photos of this strange mixture of cars are available.

By mid-1947, the OSA was better organized and the roofs and fenders came off of the cars. (Those who wanted to race with tops ran in OSA's coupe division that year.) By 1948 the OSA was running full fields of seasoned track roadsters and started to get some national publicity in Hot Rod Magazine.

Early in 1948 promoter Ed Otto from the East Coast approached OSA with the idea of taking the group's roadsters to New York and the New England states. He wanted to schedule racing five or six nights a week. Just what happened to the venture is unknown but, at any rate, it didn't happen.

Perhaps it was Ed Otto who helped link the Ohio Speedway Association with NASCAR. The roadsters were a form of stock car so NASCAR's interest is somewhat logical. Perhaps there were visions of a national roadster circuit? Early in 1948, the OSA and NASCAR began to co-sanction the roadster races. Well known racing writer and columnist, Russ Catlin appeared on the scene and began writing about the OSA-NASCAR. The races got very good publicity in *National Speed Sports News* and in other racing publications. The good publicity quickly turned to bad publicity. In just a few months Tony Banick, Mike Lesick, Bobby Fissle and Eddie Dean were killed in OSA-NASCAR races in Ohio. NASCAR quietly dropped their arrangement with the OSA.

It is strange that NASCAR chose to hook up with the Ohio Speedway Association. While they had a few good cars and drivers, they were not a strong group. The Mutual Racing Association would have been a far better choice or even a couple of California roadster organizations. Most likely it was a matter of geography—OSA was close to NASCAR racing in New York.

Thanks to Cliff Coryea of Sharpsville, Pennsylvania for most of the information in this sidebar.

Bob James was one of the stars of the Ohio Speedway Association. He is shown here at Shady Bowl in a car that is not his regular OSA ride. (Gail Alloway Collection)

Steve Lesick won a lot of OSA races. This photo was probably taken at Marion and it may or may not be an OSA sanctioned race. Engine is a Ford Six. (Gail Alloway Collection)

This 1948 Ohio Speedway Association program cover also carries the familiar NASCAR logo. (Jim Lukas Collection)

Tex Shackleford at Shady Bowl in 1950. (Gail Alloway Collection)

Chuck Farquar smiles from the Harley Pulfer Ford Six. This car ran in several Little 500s. (Gail Alloway Collection)

This is 1950 at Shady Bowl. Bobby Stokes is the driver of the Sherman Van Dyke Ford Six. (Gail Alloway Collection)

Doc Ashbaugh in the Johnny Bond Oldsmobile 88 powered car. This powerful, but heavy, engine was rare in track roadsters and, in general, did not perform too well. (Gail Alloway Collection)

Bob King is in the Jim Mullinix Merc at Shady Bowl. Not much protection for the driver in this roadster. (Gail Alloway Collection)

June of 1951 at New Bremen. This is the very neat Bernie Santo V8. Person in the photo is unknown. (Gail Alloway Collection)

Lining up at Shady Bowl. Outside on the front row is Bill Morgan in his own #5—other drivers are not known (Santo Collection)

Red Renner is pictured in the Rhonemus V8. This is Dayton in about 1947. (Zane Howell Collection)

This is the Tom Cherry roadster as a sprint car. Looks like this is an AARA sprint car race but at least one roadster is running. New Bremen in late 1954. (Gail Alloway Collection)

Jim Breese in George Bayman's Chrysler. It is 1950—location unknown. (Gail Alloway Collection)

Left–George Place leads at Landeck. Following, in order, are Don Jones, Speedy Rucker and Bud Claypool in his own Buick. (Herman Mox Collection)

Below–Bobby Lyon is leading and that's Bill Morgan in #5. Car #55 is the Cecil Adams V8 with Les Dancer at the wheel. (Herman Mox Collection)

This is the Bayman Chrysler in 1951 at New Bremen. A new body and the driver is Carl Rockwood. With all those exhaust headers, the Chrysler must be a straight eight. (Gail Alloway Collection)

Paul Hooper usually drove this car. Owner, Emmet Young rigged a flip back body so the car would be easier to work on. (Herman Mox Collection)

Did they call this the Barn Turn at Landeck? Doc McDonald is in the neat looking #53 Model T. Bob Wilson is in #11. (Herman Mox Collection)

These are the men behind the successful small town racing at Landeck. Left to right: Leo Bonifas, landowner, Mike Kill, promoter, Amos Place, Buckeye president, Don Jones and Tim Rhode. (Jack Hardesty Collection)

Action at Landeck with the corn fields in the background. Speedy Rucker leading with Walt Lear on the outside. In the center is the Frank Guda-Kunst roadster powered by a World War II Cadillac V8 M5 Tank engine. (Herman Mox Collection)

There is a good crowd on hand for this 1949 race at Landeck. The track had no lights so all races were run on Sunday afternoons. (Herman Mox Collection)

The cars head into the first turn at Landeck. The leader is Bob Wilson and that is Don Jones in second place. (Herman Mox Collection)

Bobby Lyon in #33 chases an unknown driver in what appears to be pretty much a street rod. (Herman Mox Collection)

Oklahoma

This is June 11, 1939 at the Tulsa Fairgrounds. The crowd, at 25 cents each, is apparently "normal" (Joe Stroud Collection)

Almost the entire prewar roadster racing in Oklahoma was in Tulsa. The main problem was that there was too much of it.

Racing got started in 1938 with out-and-out jalopies that were billed as "Junk Cars." These cars started racing at Devils Bowl—a track at 21st and Yale Streets. The racing was on an off-road track with lots of dust. Much of the pre-race publicity each week centered around, "Promoter Don Onley will be putting 100,000 gallons of water on the track." Cars entered could be claimed for $100—a fee that was later reduced to $50. The races drew crowds reported as up to 4800 but purses were in the $100-200 range. Late in the 1938 season, two classes of races were held with the claiming limit most likely being increased for the faster cars. It is probable that the faster cars ran on a different track and that these cars were track roadsters.

At the same time the junk cars were running at Devils Bowl, another track was opened north of Tulsa. This was called the De Luxe Junk Car Track—seems like a slight contradiction of terms! Clarence Merritt was one of the drivers here and he'll show up later driving roadsters. For a time in 1939, a Hazard Junk Car Track also operated in Tulsa—hard to say if anything like track roadsters ran at Hazard and De Luxe.

Late in 1938 Devils Bowl racer Ray Cox refused to sell his car when it was claimed. This must have been one of the faster cars—the amount of the claiming fee is unknown but Cox was promptly banned from Devils Bowl. In a move a bit like the present Indy car mess Cox went across the street, rented the Oklahoma State Fairgrounds racetrack and began promoting roadster races. Here the cars were first billed as just plain "Auto Races, then "Jalopy Cars" and later on as stock cars—they were track roadsters. Racing got off to a slow start in 1938, as there were only five cars at one race. In 1939, things were a little better with better fields supplemented by occasional visitors from Kansas. Like at Devils Bowl dusty track conditions constantly plagued the promoter Ray Cox and the racers. Pre-race publicity again stresses that "the track will be heavily watered." At one race "water facilities which had been arranged fell through at the last moment" and the local newspaper reported a "dust storm at the Tulsa Fairgrounds." Later in the summer of 1939, the track was oiled but this helped very little.

Clyde Greever was one of the more successful drivers at Tulsa in 1938 and 1939. (Joe Stroud Collection)

Clarence Merritt won a lot of roadster races at Tulsa in 1939 and went on to win local midget championships in 1942 and 1945. (Joe Stroud Collection)

Roy Coleman had an OHV four banger in his O'Hara Speedway car. Coleman did very well in the big cars and midgets. (Perry Kratchmer Collection)

Roy Coleman fights for control after losing a wheel at O'Hara. His mount appears to be closer to a sprint car than a roadster. Number 13 is probably Tommy Goodman. (Perry Kratchmer Collection)

The publicity about poor track conditions was not good and the crowds are believed to be in the 100 to 200 range. Jimmy Campbell took over the promotion and, a bit later, raised the admission price from 25 to 35 cents so maybe things got a bit better late in the 1939 season. Drivers at the fairgrounds track included Harry West, who later won a lot of IMCA big car races, and Clarence Merritt, a future Oklahoma midget star. There is no evidence of roadster racing of any kind in Tulsa in 1940 and 1941. Crowds had dropped off at Devils Bowl, De Luxe was apparently a short-lived operation and it is not surprising that the fairgrounds track did not operate.

There may have been some prewar roadster racing in Oklahoma City. Several drivers from that city competed at Tulsa and maybe a track operated in their hometown.

After World War II, there was roadster racing at O'Hara Speedway in Oklahoma City. Racing started there in the summer of 1946 with the roadsters being billed as "Junk Car Races." Although most were primitive, these were quite definitely track roadsters. There were a few A-V8s running, some hopped up Chevies and Roy Colman ran a Four Port Riley in his roadster that probably also competed as a sprint car. Jack Randel ran a slightly unusual V8 60. (See Sidebar) While the O'Hara track was a bit off level, it was more of an oval than an off-road course. Purses at O'Hara are unknown but a main event winner could probably take home about $100. The only published data on purses comes from a news story on driver Pat McCleary who was paid $86 for a win and three second places. Sadly, this item came from a story on McCleary's death at O'Hara the following week.

At about the same time at least three other tracks were running "Junk Cars" in Oklahoma City. One was Devils Bowl and it was an off-road course. There was another track at an amusement park and a third northwest of the city. At this track a car went into the crowd and hurt a number of people seriously.

In Tulsa, there is no evidence that the roadsters tried again at the fairgrounds. Tulsa roadster racing turns up at the Mohawk Speedway in 1949. Once again the cars were "Junk Cars"—Oklahoma promoters must have figured that "Junk" brought in the fans. Wayne Servaes won most of the races at Mohawk in a very nice looking car that apparently also ran on the street. Once again, there was dissension in the ranks for the Tulsa racers and, in 1950, New Mohawk Speedway was opened nearby. It wasn't long before the coupes were running at both tracks and the roadsters were on the way out. One photo shows the coupes and roadsters running in the same race—scary!

In other parts of Oklahoma there was some roadster racing in the late 1940s. Most of this was in Woodward and Don Baxter of Woodward documents it in an unpublished Hot Rod Racing History in Woodward, Oklahoma. Although a relatively small community the Woodward group ran successful races with a variety of home-built cars. This racing went on from 1947 until 1950 despite two fatal accidents.

It seemed likely that if there were roadster racing in Woodward that there would also be racing in other smaller Oklahoma towns. Research turned up lots of stock car racing but no roadsters. A few roadsters were built in these towns but they raced elsewhere—usually in Kansas.

FROM INDY TO THE ROADSTERS

There are 80 or more roadster drivers who made it to the Indianapolis 500. There is only one who reversed the procedure. This is John Boling who ran at Indy in 1920 and 1931 and then showed up at a Tulsa roadster race in 1938.

A July 17, 1938 clipping from a Tulsa newspaper indicates that "John Boling, twice a contestant in the Indianapolis Speedway race, will be a dangerous contender." The headline of the clipping refers to the "Junk Derby" but it appears that two classes of cars were running at the races. Let's assume that Boling ran something akin to a track roadster. There was no follow up to the story so Boling may or may not have been a "dangerous contender."

Just on the basis of his Indy career John Boling is somewhat of a mystery figure. It is doubtful if any other driver ran in only two races eleven years apart. In 1920 he qualified a car with a 179 cubic inch, six cylinder, Brett motor at 81.85 MPH—one of the slowest in the 23-car field. He was awarded 11th place in the race at a speed of around 66-MPH. There is no record of him even appearing at Indianapolis until 1931 when he qualified a Morton and Brett Special with a 226 cubic inch eight cylinder engine at 102.860 MPH. This was about midway in the field. Boling was out on the seventh lap with connecting rod problems. Just where and if Boling raced from 1920 until 1938 is another mystery.

John Boling and riding mechanic Buddy Boles are pictured at Indianapolis is 1931. The engine may be a hopped up Chrysler Eight. (Bruce Craig Collection)

The New Mohawk Speedway in 1950 and the coupes are racing. There is a roadster on the outside of the tangle so both types of cars must have raced in the same events. (Lew Jarrett Photo—Mark Downing Collection)

Wayne Servaes (pronounced "Service") was one of Tulsa's top roadster drivers. Number 17 is his first track roadster. (Mark Downing Collection)

Marvin Johnson gets a bit wide at O'Hara and kicks up some dust. (Perry Kratchmer Collection)

A couple of roadsters do battle at Tulsa's Mohawk Speedway in 1949. That's Marvin Trowbridge on the outside. (Downing-Trowbridge Collection)

Wayne Servaes in action later in 1949. This car is obviously a street rod and is owned by a Mr. Ramsey. Servaes won races in this car. (Lew Jarrett Photo—Mark Downing Collection)

Wayne Servaes accepts congratulations after another win at Mohawk Speedway. (Lew Jarrett Photo—Mark Downing Collection)

POSITIVE IDENTIFICATIONS!

Even rarer than finding nice clear photos like the ones shown here is finding correct identifications. The photos were found without IDs and very nearly stayed that way. Racing writer and historian, Galen Kurth wrote an article appealing for help with roadster identifications and arranged to have it (along with the photos) published in the Oklahoma City State Fair Speedway program. In the stands that night was Mrs. Paul Cockrell who came forward and provided what are certainly the most positive IDs in the book. Mrs. Cockrell is still a race fan after all these years and is a regular at the State Fair Speedway. She added that her late husband, Paul, Eddie Carmichael and Bob Green all went on to a successful career in the midgets and sprints.

Paul Cockrell

Eddie Carmichael

Bob Green

Bobby Laden

Bud Robinson

Another Wayne Servaes roadster. As is obvious from the trophies this car was a winner. (Downing-Servaes Collection)

Mohawk Speedway in Tulsa in 1949. Jerry Riggs is shown in a V8 owned by Wayne Servaes. (Lew Jarrett Photo-Mark Downing Collection)

Track personnel attend to an injured driver at O'Hara Speedway in a 1946 race. (Perry Kratchmer Collection)

Car #61 cranks out a fast lap at O'Hara Speedway in 1946. Spectators had an excellent, if a bit unsafe, view at this Oklahoma City track, (Perry Kratchmer Collection)

BACKWARDS

It is said all too often in this book that most racers preferred to follow rather than lead—off the track that is. The great majority of roadster racers simply copied the other guy. Not so with Jack Randel in Oklahoma City. He ran his engine backwards!

The accompanying photo was found about three years ago with no identification. Thanks mostly to Perry Kratchmer in Oklahoma City pieces of the puzzle have been partly found and put together. It was established Jack Randel was the builder and driver of the car and that it ran at O'Hara Speedway in 1946. Close examination shows the engine to be a V8-60. Randel has his helmet on backwards so the photo is probably a publicity shot for the backward engine.

The question remains—just how did Randel do it? Reversing the porting on V8 engines is not all that unusual but it can be assumed that Jack Randel had something less than Penske-type technology behind him in Oklahoma City in 1946. The best guess of a dozen or so flathead "experts" is that Randel did not actually reverse the engine rotation. How about if he simply put the cam in 180 degrees off of the timing mark? Wouldn't that change the valve timing so that the engine would run with reverse porting? Anybody out there have a V8 apart so this can be checked out?

Jack Randel went to a lot of work to run this V8-60 backwards. There is no record of how the car performed. (Perry Kratchmer Collection)

Jack Randel is to be admired for his innovation. If he was trying to keep the engine from overheating this probably worked. Unfortunately, even under the best of circumstances, a V8-60 would not be competitive in a track roadster.

Ontario

There was a bit of roadster racing in Ontario but it seems that most of it was with US cars and drivers. Oddly, although there are a few familiar names, very little is known about the US racers.

On July 10, 1948 Pinecrest Speedway opened north of Toronto. Competing in the opening program were seven sprint cars, a few midgets and enough roadsters to run two heats and an eight lap feature. There were a few local roadsters but most were from Buffalo, New York. It is believed that the stock cars quickly took over at Pinecrest so, odds are, there was only the one roadster race. Roadsters may have raced at Norwich and at a later Pinecrest Speedway but these were probably full fendered cars that ran with the coupes. It is known that the cars were driven to the tracks and that cage rollbars were required.

In the Ottawa area there were roadster races at Landsdow Park in about 1950. Nothing is known about these races.

Starting in 1948 roadster races were run at Windsor Speedway in Windsor. The track was only a few miles from Detroit so the majority of the cars and drivers came from that city. A 1948 program lists some familiar names like Al Miller, Iggy Katona, Bob Rogers and Gervaise Umek but only two Canadians—Merle Lanlois and Edgar Loree. It appears that there was a series of races in 1948 and, almost certainly, there were spot roadster races at Windsor up until about 1952. Possibly, in later years, more Canadian cars and drivers competed.

The only other area in Ontario that may have had roadster racing is Thunder Bay. This is adjacent to Minnesota but a long haul from the Minneapolis area where most of the roadster racing took place in that state. There were three tracks in the Thunder Bay area around 1950 and there could have been roadster racing but, surely, there would not be enough local cars for a race. Minnesota research turned up a few vague references to "a swing up through Canada" but nothing definite surfaced. With the ravages of time on memories, it very well could be that the cars involved were sprint cars and not roadsters. It is known that the IMCA ran races in Canada on their fair circuits.

Left–The roadsters line up for a race at Pinecrest Speedway near Toronto. Most of the cars are from Buffalo, New York but nothing is known of their activities in that city. (Dave Boon Collection)

Roadster action at Pinecrest Speedway on opening day July 10, 1948. This is almost certainly the only true roadster race held at Pinecrest. (Dave Boon Collection)

A couple of roadsters battle at Pinecrest in 1948. Car #11 appears to be a street rod. It is not known if these were Canadian cars or if they were from the US. (Dave Boon Collection)

Marion Sroka is shown at Windsor Speedway in about 1950. Like most of the drivers at Windsor Sroka was from Detroit. (Larry Wendt Collection)

Bob Rogers was another US driver who competed at Windsor Speedway. The engine type is unknown. (Larry Wendt Collection)

Oregon

A four banger (#4) lines up at Portland in 1946. This car certainly raced in prewar roadster events in Oregon and/or Washington. The driver is Johnny Gorman. (Jay Koch Collection)

It is known that there was pre-World War II roadster racing in Oregon but that's about it. The races were almost certainly at the Gresham Speedbowl a few miles outside of Portland.

After the war the Oregon Roadster Racing Association was organized before any races were held. (In 1947 the name was changed to the Roadster Racing Association of Oregon—nobody knows why) Some of the members had raced roadsters in Washington and it was felt that a formal organization would put them in a better position to deal with promoters. The first event, at Portland Speedway in late 1946, was a series of timed laps during a sprint car race. A few weeks later the roadsters were back for their own race and there were 10,000 people in the grandstand. Bob Donker won the race and must have taken a lot of money home to Seattle.

Midget driver Frankie McGowen won most of the races in the remainder of the 1946 season in Pop Koch's Model A-Lincoln Zephyr V-12. This is the only record of this boat-anchor heavy V-12 performing well in the roadsters. Koch had removed the flywheel and clutch and had it in a lightweight chassis. Most of the competition was running basically street roadsters.

By the time the 1947 season opened the Oregon cars were a lot closer to true track roadsters. In May of that year a visit by southern California hot shots Jack McGrath and Manny Ayulo informed the Oregonians that there was still room for improvement. McGrath and Ayulo knocked a couple of seconds off of track records so it was back to the drawing (copying) board.

For the next several seasons the Oregon roadster racers kept busy with their own events at Portland Speedway and in other Oregon cities. Except for a period in 1950, there was cooperation with the Washington roadster group and the two organizations exchanged cars freely. In general, the Oregon cars were a bit faster—especially Len Sutton in the Pop Koch built Rolla Vollstedt Merc. For most of the roadster era there were races at Seattle's Aurora Stadium and a number of Oregon cars would make the 180-mile tow northward to compete.

By about 1951 it was the same old story as the stock cars took over the racetracks and the fans dollars. Unlike in most areas the Oregon roadsters managed to keep their organization together and to hold races. A few of the roadsters became sprint cars but the owners would put on roadster bodies and support the Roadster Racing Association of Oregon events. Most of these races (1951 to 1954) were at Salem, indications are the crowds and purs-

Frankie McGowen is in Pop Koch's Model A-Lincoln V-12 at Portland in 1946. Note that there is no firewall and Mc Gowen's legs are visible. (Jack Greiner Photo)

Midget star Gordy Youngstrom drove this '32 Ford convertible in the first Portland roadster race. This was a very rare model—only about 500 of these cars were built. (Jack Greiner Photo)

Action in the first Portland race in 1946. That is Len Sutton leading—strictly street rods. (Jay Koch Collection)

One of Len Sutton's first races ended early as he spun into the wild roses that lined the backstretch at Portland. This is Sutton's street roadster. (Jay Koch Collection)

Frankie McGowen leads in an early Portland race. Phil Foubert is driving the very low car on the outside. (Jay Koch Collection)

Bob Gregg at Portland in 1947. This car dubbed the "Little Red Wagon" won a lot of races. (Jack Greiner Photo)

A group of roadsters prepare to take to the track at Portland Speedway in 1946. (Golden Wheels Collection)

Jack Greiner raced this neat looking street rod in 1947. In '46, it could have been a winner but not so in 1947. (Jack Greiner Collection)

es were not too bad.

In 1955, time caught up to the Oregon roadsters and the last race was held on June 18 of that year. This was at Salem and to Ernie Koch went the honor of winning the last roadster race in Oregon.

The Oregon roadsters produced some great drivers. Heading the list would have to be Len Sutton who went on to Indy and finished second in 1962. George Amick, who finished second in the 1958 Indy 500, got his start in the Oregon roadsters. Ernie Koch was a winner in the roadsters and later drove the Rolla Vollstedt Offy in Champ car races. Other fine drivers were Bill Hyde, Palmer Crowell, Bob Gregg, Max Humm, Darmond Moore, Andy Wilson, Howard Osborne, Ben Eyerly, Frankie Mc Gowen, Russ Gilbertson and midget ace Gordy Youngstrom.

An Oregon roadster history would not be complete without mention of starter Pat Vidan. Vidan's talents were evident from the beginning and it didn't take him long to get to Indy where he was Chief Starter for 15 years.

The field heads into the first turn at Portland. This is probably in 1948. (Jay Koch Collection)

Walt Begaul was fatally injured in this car at Portland in 1948. The car hit the wall head-on at full speed. (Jack Greiner Collection)

Driver Andy Wilson (left) and owner Don Waters smile after a main event win at Portland Speedway. The Bob Gregg driven #1 is in the background

Crewmen tie down Don Waters' roadster for a trip to Seattle in 1948. Few roadster racers traveled so stylishly. (Jack Greiner Photo)

STREET TO TRACK TO STREET

In the early days of postwar roadster racing a lot of nice looking street hot rods took to the speedways. Few survived to return to the streets. An exception was Tom Story's A-V8 in Portland.

The problem with street roadsters on the track was the things that made them look nice were just not required on the track. A fancy nose and grill could add to an overheating problem. A nice upholstery job was added weight. On many roadsters unnecessary and "in the way" parts were rudely and crudely removed. At this point, it was "What the hell, let's chop it up some more and go racing."

Tom Story raced the car at Portland Speedway in early 1947 and Jim Martin did the driving. There is no record of how the car did but it should have been competitive for the first few races. The Oregon roadsters were still in the transition stage so the clutch and transmission in the street rod would not be a big handicap. One thing in the car's favor was that the nice looking nose had a big opening to cool the V8. Had the opening been smaller who knows what would have been done in "the heat of battle"? It is probable that Story did not run the car for long and he was lucky that it was not wrecked.

Tom Story's bodyworking talents were obvious in the nose of the car before it took to the track. Back on the street, Story worked on the remainder of the body and created a show class car.

Tom Story, in the passenger's seat, and Jim Martin get ready to head for Portland Speedway in 1947. (Dick Martin Collection)

It is 1948 and the Tom Story roadster is back on the street with a beautiful (and hard to photograph) black paint job. (Jack Greiner Photo)

Jim Martin is lined up for a race at Portland Speedway. Here he gets last minute advice from owner Tom Story. Like maybe, "Please don't bend that pretty nose"? (Dick Martin Collection)

Midget driver Frankie McGowen was back in the roadsters in 1950. Here he gets ready to win a Portland feature in the Don Turner Merc. (Jack Greiner Photo)

Don Porter gets set to qualify Bob Smith's (at left) Merc at Portland Speedway. Porter died in a sprint car crash a few years later. (Jack Greiner Photo)

Bob Gregg drove this nice looking roadster at Portland Meadows. Gregg had a long and successful career in Pacific Northwest racing. (Jack Greiner Photo)

Palmer Crowell was one of the better Oregon roadster racers. He's shown at a Portland Meadows 100-mile sprint car race in 1954. Crowell competed in USAC midget and Silver Crown events until the 1990s. (Don Radbruch Photo)

Len Sutton won close to 100 Oregon and Washington main events. He was a winner in the midgets, sprints and, later on, in the Indy cars. (Jay Koch Collection)

This is 1950 at the half-mile dirt Portland Meadows track. Max Humm is the driver and dirty owner Don Waters has just changed the rear end gears. (Jack Greiner Photo)

Len Sutton and Ernie Koch in #1 get ready for a race at Portland. Sutton was a three time Oregon champion and Koch won the title twice. (Jay Koch Collection)

Car owner Rolla Vollstedt is shown in his Horning 12-Port GMC. Vollstedt later fielded champ dirt cars and Indy cars. (Jay Koch Collection)

Salem in 1952 and Ben Eyerly is driving the Jack Greiner Merc. He has just run over an infield marker and bent the belly pan. (Jack Greiner Collection)

No, this is not for real. It is a Bill Hyde built "gag car" at Salem in 1950. (Nancy Radbruch Collection)

Jack Greiner's girlfriend, Rolleen, is shown with his Merc at Salem in 1949. Rolleen soon became Mrs. Greiner and the two are still together. (Jack Greiner Photo)

The very potent Rolla Vollstedt GMC. For a time Vollstedt experimented with floatless carburetors. This is at Jantzen Beach in Portland and Len Sutton was the driver. (Jack Greiner Photo)

The last roadster race in Oregon—Salem on June 18, 1955. In #3 is Ed Kane, #55 Jerry Dundin, #93 Ben Eyerly and #23 is John Fugitt. (Jack Greiner Collection)

The lineup on April 22, 1951 at Portland. Row 1—Ike Hanks and George Amick, row 2—Bob Donker and Darmond Moore, row 3—Ernie Koch and California visitor Lemonine Frey. (Jack Greiner Collection)

Pennsylvania

Pennsylvania roadster racing began in the early 1930s in the southeastern part of the state. From historian Carl Sweigart comes information on one of the first races—a special event at an AAA race promoted by the legendary Ralph Hankinson. This was at Landisville and the ten-lap race was no doubt billed as a stock car event. The competing cars were all stripped roadsters and there is little doubt that most had modified engines. Some very good future big car drivers took part in this race. Ottis Stein and Ted Nyquist both had Chrysler "70" roadsters and Mark Light had a very hot Model A. Unfortunately, the race ended in disaster as Light's car broke a right front wheel and crashed. Light had a rider with him in the car—his name was Stager and he was fatally injured. This soured Hankinson on the stock cars-roadsters and he refused to help promote further races.

Mel Weidner is pictured at Zeller's Grove in 1948. The body modifications have not done much for the looks of the Model A. (Les King-Larry Sullivan Collection)

Red Deiter at Zeller's Grove in 1947. Deiter was killed in a roadster at Williams Grove. (Carl Sweigart Collection)

Later in the 1930s and early '40s there were a few roadster races held at towns like Schuykill Haven and Lebanon. There was another fatality at Lebanon in 1940 when Howard Evans was killed in a crash—this was the last race ever held in this town.

In about 1940 a series of roadster races was held at Lattimer Valley. Thanks to John Rollin, who promoted the races, some information is available. No actual roadster group was formed but 16 to 18 cars would race for purses of around $135 with $35 to win the main. Overhead valve heads were not permitted but the sky was the limit on flatheads and bodies could be stripped to near nothing.

In addition to the previously mentioned oval track racing, there were

Chuck Feltenburger in one of the very fast Ray Madera V8s. The rollbar is made from a steel farm equipment wheel—a common practice in Pennsylvania. (Carl Sweigart Collection)

primitive roadsters that ran off-road courses in dozens of small Pennsylvania towns. Typical of this type of racing was "Satan's Speedway of Death" in Sykesville.

Since there was no real roadster group in existence postwar Pennsylvania racing started out in a rather unorganized fashion. In 1946 races were held at Zeller's Grove near Myerstown. There were a few prewar roadsters plus whatever showed up—coupes, pickups, big cars and who knows what. This sort of racing went on for over a year until, recognizing the need for a proper organization and rules, the Keystone Roadster Racing Association was formed in 1948. Keystone expanded roadster racing to several towns in southeastern Pennsylvania and soon they were racing several times a week. Drivers such as Bob Rolland, Vince Conrad, Ringy Lloyd, Red Dieter, Pat Patterson and Bob Eby competed for purses

This mud-spattered roadster and poster advertise an early race at Lattimer. No mention of the purse but odds are it was less than $150. (Lynn Paxton Collection)

Mel Kreiser in another one of the Ray Madera A-V8s. Madera was president of Keystone as well as the owner of two winning cars. (Carl Sweigart Collection)

Bobby Rolland at Zeller's Grove in 1947. This car looks as though it may have raced before WW II. (Carl Sweigart Collection)

Bob Eby in the Dutch Heilman Model B. Eby won the 1948 Keystone Roadster Racing championship in this car. (Carl Sweigart Collection)

that averaged around $500.

As it is today Williams Grove was the premier track in the area and for the most part sanctioned AAA sprint car races. A few roadster races were held there but for some reason the sanctioning body was the Eastern Roadster Association from neighboring Virginia. In 1948 and 1949 "National Championship" roadster races took place at Williams Grove. Both races attracted stellar fields of roadsters from all over the eastern part of the United States. Dick Frazier from Indiana was the class of the field but, on both occasions, ran into trouble in the fifty lap main events and the winners were Willy Stromquist from Chicago and Indiana's Smokey Stover.

No identification on this youngster at Lattimer. Did he grow up to be somebody we all know? (Lynn Paxton Collection)

George Donavan is shown at Zeller's Grove in 1947. The engine is a Model B flathead. (Carl Sweigart Collection)

Pat Patterson at Zeller's Grove in 1948. Since a number of flathead Model As were running, they must have been competitive. (Les King-Larry Sullivan Collection)

This appears to be prewar "Barrelhoop" car that has been fitted with a V8 engine. The driver is unknown. (Les King-Larry Sullivan Collection)

The Eastern Racing Association wished all the fans happy holidays with this card in 1949. The driver in the middle (black uniform) looks like Roy Prosser—what was he doing in Pennsylvania. (Vince Conrad Collection)

Vince Conrad in his first track roadster—looks like a converted street A-V8. As of a few years ago Conrad was playing in a rock band. (Vince Conrad Collection)

Blackie Reider at Zeller's Grove in 1948. Reider later drove stock cars and modifieds. (Carl Sweigart Collection)

This advertisement is from either 1947 or 1948. (Vince Conrad Collection)

PITTSBURGH

Thanks to western Pennsylvania racing historian Dave Burt there is some information available on roadster racing in the Pittsburgh area.

Roadster racing in the Pittsburgh area started with stripped jalopies on off-road tracks. There were tracks at Large, Bakerstown and New Kessington. The track at New Kessington was covered with oil and silver paint to keep the dust down—the EPA would love this sort of thing today!

The jalopies soon acquired bodies and hopped up engines to become track roadsters. Instrumental in this changeover were drivers like Bill "Pappy" Kessler, Herb Scott and Lee Stover. Kessler helped form the Pittsburgh Roaring Roadsters Club (PRRA). This group probably started racing at New Kessington Speedway northeast of Pittsburgh in 1948. In about 1950 Bill Kessler helped build Penn Speedway and it is believed there was weekly roadster racing there for two seasons.

There is no evidence that the Pittsburgh Roaring Roadsters raced at tracks other than Penn and Kessington. Perhaps the reason for this was the strict "Blue Laws" in the area. This prohibited racing on Sundays and would just about rule out racing on country fair ovals.

New Kessington Speedway in 1949. Bill Guthrie drove this car. (Dave Burt Collection)

Buddy O'Connor drove the Greenfield Special. O'Connor raced from the 1930s to around 1970 and is one of the better-known western Pennsylvania drivers. (Dave Burt Collection)

This New Kessington car was driven by Herb Scott who, later in his career, won over 500 stock car features. Scott was a ten time Pittsburgh Racing Association champion. (Dave Burt Collection)

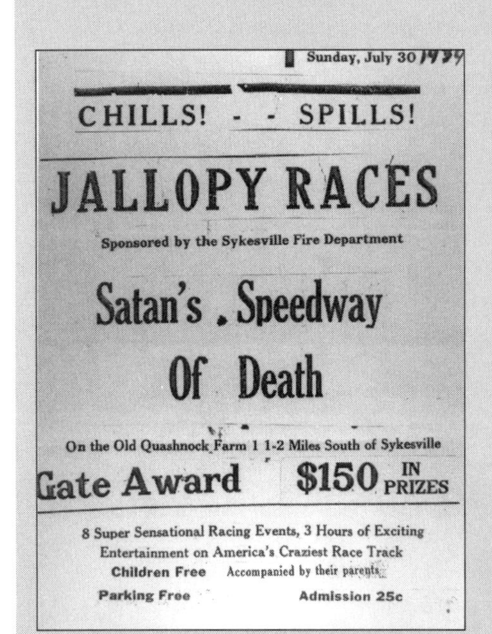

This track was one of several that ran jallopy-roadster races in the Du Bois area during the late 1930s. (Norman Henry Collection)

The Quashnock Farm Muddy Track in 1939. The flagman is none other than thirteen time Indy vet Deacon Litz. (Tom Donahue Collection)

Norman Henry is shown with his Chevy jallopy in 1939. He was a main event winner at Satan's Bowl of Death. (Norman Henry Collection)

This is Tom Donahue at Satan's Speedway of Death in 1939. That is a 1924 Star roadster. (Tom Donahue Collection)

Left–The Norman Henry Chevy was a lot neater than most cars that ran in off road jallopy races. Most cars were stripped to near nothing but Henry ran a full roadster body. (Norman Henry Collection)

This is either the Salem or London Mines track near Du Bois. Andy Durkin is shown with his stripped down Model A roadster. (Andy Durkin Collection)

Du Bois is a town of around 8000 in western Central Pennsylvania. It is a hundred miles from any other known roadster-racing venue. Despite this isolation, the Du Bois area had an active roadster-racing program from 1939 until the early 1950s.

It all started at Sykesville, a few miles south of Du Bois, when the local fire department sponsored races at Satan's Speedway of Death. This was an off road course with bumps, holes and water hazards. The cars were stripped roadsters and engine modifications were probably allowed and/or tolerated. Norman Henry was one of the racers and he built a neat looking Chevy roadster. The state of the art technology for the Satan racers was knobby rear tires and a sack of sand in the trunk for traction. Henry was one of the more successful drivers and won at least one main event. Despite sponsorship from his dad, the local Oldsmobile and Chevy dealer, Norman Henry quit racing after a dozen or so races. The reason is all too familiar to today's racers— "It was too expensive to keep the jalopy in running condition."

The Satan's Speedway of Death drew good crowds so it soon had competition from three other tracks in the Du Bois area. It is probable that one or more of these tracks operated until WW II stopped racing.

Ted Wells did a good job of building his Salem car in 1947—note the double shocks. The angle of that front "wing" does appear a bit severe. (Tom Donahue Collection)

An early version of the Smoky Gearhart supercharged car. It is a '34 Plymouth roadster with a Ford front end. (Gearhart Collection)

This Smoky Gearhart car ran second in a 1949 sprint car race at the Gateway Fairgrounds in Du Bois. Gearhart is at the left. (Gearhart Collection)

Jim Beers tangled with a tree during roadster races at the Gateway Fairgrounds. Despite the bandages, Beers is in better shape than his car. (Gearhart Collection)

Tom Donahue raced this flathead Model A at the Gateway Fairgrounds in Du Bois. (Tom Donahue Collection)

The lineup at Gateway Fairgrounds in 1947. Tom Donahue is on the pole with the Smoky Gearhart car right behind. (Tom Donahue Collection)

Right–Another view of the Gateway cars—with a good crowd on hand. Despite the muddy looking track, dust was a problem. (Tom Donahue Collection)

In 1947 jalopy-roadster racing resumed in the Du Bois area and thanks to Les Smiley of that city information is available on these races. Racing started on two off-road courses—the Salem and London Mines tracks. At first most of the cars were stripped Model A Fords—perhaps some were veterans of the prewar races. It wasn't long before better cars started racing. It also wasn't long before the racers wanted to go faster and compete on the half miler at the Du Bois Gateway Fairgrounds (aka City Park or Driving Park).

Not too many races were held on the oval before the city fathers (and a nearby hospital) found reason to object to the noise and dust. Smoky Gearhart built one of the better roadsters to run at Gateway. It was a '33 Plymouth roadster with a later model bored out Chrysler Spitfire engine. This engine sported a supercharger from a 1936 Graham Paige and a homemade camshaft. The Gearhart machine more than held its own against the more conventional V8s and hopped up four bangers.

Perhaps Smoky Gearhart's finest moment came when a sprint car race was scheduled at Gateway Fairgrounds. A car shortage developed and the roadsters were invited to run. With Frank Radaker (?) at the wheel the Gearhart #13 took second place in a field of (Les Smiley's words)—"hifalutin Offys."

Dick Frazier and the Hack Winninger Merc showed up at the 1948 Williams Grove championship race and outqualified the field by three seconds. Mechanical problems kept him from running away with the fifty lap main event. (Carl Sweigart Collection).

Clarence Prutzman drove this V8 at Zeller's Grove. No doubt, the door was removed to give the driver elbowroom but it looks scary. (Les King-Larry Sullivan Collection)

Norm McCarthy from Ohio at Williams Grove in 1949. Looks like somebody got superstitious and changed #13 to #1/3. (Carl Sweigart Collection)

This photo of Jimmy Delcamp provides a good view of Hilltop Speedway. This track, near Myerstown, ran roadster races for several seasons. (Delcamp Collection)

Vince Conrad at one of the Williams Grove "National Championship" races. Car owner Francis Schradin is at the left. (Vince Conrad Collection)

Johnny Duris drove this very nice looking A-V8 at Williams Grove. (Les King-Larry Sullivan Collection)

RULES AND REGULATIONS

KEYSTONE ROADSTER RACING ASSOCIATION

1436 N. NINTH STREET
READING, PA.
1948

Keystone was the dominant roadster group in southeastern Pennsylvania. It wasn't a very thick rulebook. (Vince Conrad Collection)

George Lund at Zeller's Grove. Note the lack of protection for the spectators. (Carl Sweigart Collection)

Bob James at Williams Grove in 1949. James won a lot of Ohio roadster races in this V8. (Carl Sweigart Collection)

Carl Anderson raced mostly with the Eastern Racing Association and was a champion of that group. (Carl Sweigart Collection)

Bob Nay sits very tall in a low slung roadster. This is Williams Grove in 1950. (Les King-Larry Sullivan Collection)

Jim Delcamp at Williams Grove. This photo was taken at the "National Championship" races on August 11, 1949. (Delcamp Collection—Frank Smith Photo)

Scandinavia

(Thanks to Tonas Karlsson and Per-Olof Carlsson of Sweden for all the information and the photos in this chapter)

The auto racing history of the Scandinavian countries is not well known in the United States. A few Formula One races have been run in Sweden and a number of Formula One drivers have come from various Scandinavian countries. There was, and is, lots of racing in these countries.

Per-Olof Carlsson has provided an unpublished manuscript Roadsters in Scandinavia by Tonas Karlsson. This very nicely documents the history of roadster racing—Scandinavian style.

Although racing started in the 1920s a problem for Scandinavian racers was an acute shortage of racetracks—Sweden, for instance, didn't have a permanent racetrack until 1950. There were races on dirt horse tracks, some hill climbs and, during the long winters, there were lots of nice open flat surfaces to race on—ice! Races were held on snow-plowed ice on both lakes and on the sea. Competition varied from speed runs to oval and road type courses.

Most of the roadsters that raced were street machines and the term "hot rod" is a more apt description than "track roadster." (The Swedish term for "hot rod" is, by the way, "hot rod.") Usually races were open to all comers and the fields could vary from a few Formula One (then Grand Prix) cars to stock cars, sports cars and the "specials" that would include the hot rods. Strangely enough, most of the Scandinavian specials were based on American built Ford products. The Model Ts, Model As and the V8s were just as popular with the Scandinavian hot rodders

This is an International race at Skarpnack airfield near Stockholm in 1949. A very mixed field! There are a few true track roadsters mixed in with the specials, a 500 cc rear engined car and the German Grand Prix cars up front. The car at the left was built from a wrecked Kaiser taxicab—it performed well.

This team of nice looking roadsters had backing from Swedish Chevrolet dealers. The team competed at Ramen in 1932 and won first place for the best team effort.

Finnish driver Einar Alm raced this Ford Special in Norway in 1935. He used Model T frame rails and a '32 V8 engine. The front suspension is unusual.

The Danes favored racing on oval dirt tracks. This is Arby in 1951. There are a couple of Ford specials on the outside as Jensen leads in a Ford V8 with Olson close behind in a Steyr V8.

as they were in the US.

Starting in 1931 a series of big races were held at Lake Ramen in Sweden. This was the Swedish Winter Grand Prix and the course was partly on the frozen lake and partly on narrow roads around the lake. Ford specials placed well in the first race and then, in 1932, the race was won by Olle Bennstrom in a Model A roadster with a Record head, magneto and two Swedish built carburetors. The engine put out an impressive 97 horsepower at 3000 rpm. This was a big win in a big race—Bennstrom won a lot of money, was awarded a Ford dealership and became famous overnight.

Olle Bennstrom was back in 1933 as a member of a three car Ford team. This time there was V8 power and lightweight aluminum bodies. An Alfa Romeo won at Ramen but the Fords were second and third.

During the prewar years, there were also races in Finland and Ford specials gave a good account of themselves. In Finland Einar Alm built what was very close to a track roadster. He used a Model T frame, a '32 V8 engine and an in-and-out box instead of a transmission. The body was a modified streamlined semi-coupe built of wood and sailcloth. Alm raced the car in Norway in the winter of 1935 but had so little success he had to sell his heavy-duty leather trousers to get back home.

War clouds pretty much ended racing by 1938 and it was not resumed until 1946—no new equipment would be available for several more years.

A Norwegian Model B Ford powered roadster, built from a conglomeration of assorted car parts, pretty well dominated Swedish racing during the first few years of postwar events. Arvid Johanssen and then, new owner, Arne Hinsvaerk won hill climbs, horse track races and ice events in the car. In Finland racing got underway again in 1947 and Ford V8 specials more than held their own.

In 1949, an international race was held at Skarpnack, an airfield outside of Stockholm. The field was the grandaddy of all "Run what yuh brung" races. There were a couple of European Grand Prix cars, the mostly Ford based specials, some rear engined British 500 cc cars, a couple of cars loosely based on American midgets and assorted sports cars. It was no contest as the Grand Prix cars simply played with the rest of the field.

Later in 1949 it was decided to start a special Nordic Class—all cars had to be home built and based on stock cars—hot rods! In August a race under this new formula was held at Gardemoen airfield in Norway. No Finnish cars showed up and Arnie Hinsvaerk, still winning races in his four banger, stayed home in an argument over starting money. Thure Melin won the race in his Ford V8 special.

The Scandinavian cooperation on the Nordic

Class didn't last very long. Danish and Norwegian racers quickly lost interest but the series continued in Sweden and Finland. Races were on dirt horse tracks, airport road courses and on the ice. No information is available on purses but photos show large crowds in the background. Some very good cars were built. One was constructed by Erik Lundgren. This was based on mostly Ford parts and had a V8 engine with Ardun heads. Lundgren won a lot of races.

In appearance, the Nordic Class cars were somewhat of a cross between sprint cars, roadsters and sports cars. A lot of work went into the bodies and, apparently, this was to save weight. It is almost certain that, had Model T bodies been available, somebody would have used one.

The Nordic class cars, still mostly Ford V8 based, ran until about 1955.

All photos are from Roadsters in Scandinavia by Tonas Karlsson.

Ollie Bennstrom and his #9 were part of the Ford team at Ramen, Sweden in 1933. The V8 powered specials had lightweight aluminum bodies and the engines were said to have put out 120 horsepower.

Danish driver, Robert Nelleman ran this big and heavy Ford V8 special.

Trondheim, Norway in 1937. In front is Greger Strom in what is really a Model A based big car. Arvid Johansen is in the Model A roadster. The engine is a hopped up flathead A.

The first Swedish hot rod? This "Darek Ford" reached a speed of 84 MPH on frozen Lake Varpan in 1924. A very creditable speed for a Model T Ford.

South Dakota

Roadster racing in South Dakota began in the early 1930s when a roadster group was formed in the Sioux Falls area. Almost nothing is known about this group. It appears that big car racer Jimmy Wood converted his Chevy racecar to a roadster and ran with the group. Wood's career is quite well documented but nothing on the roadster racing turns up. Either roadster racing was short lived in the Sioux Falls area or the roadster drivers didn't like Jimmy Wood winning the money. Who knows?

Post war roadster racing began in Huron in 1948. This was an outgrowth of a street roadster club called, of all things, The Snails. This group, along with local service clubs, was behind most of the roadster racing in South Dakota but no actual racing organization was formed. In South Dakota, roadster races were held at Huron, Glenwood, Mitchell, Gettysburg, Aberdeen, Winner, Sioux Falls and possibly other towns. Most of the races were strictly for South Dakota cars and the car counts were low—probably eight to twelve cars.

An exception was a race on Labor Day weekend, 1949, at Sioux Falls in the southeast corner of the state. The promoters put up a purse of $1000 for each of two races. This attracted a field of 30 cars and drivers from South Dakota, Iowa and Minnesota—there were many familiar names on the entry list. Minnesota driver Vern Kolb won every race that he was in and took home $300.

Roadster racing in South Dakota went on for several years but no champions were crowned. The top drivers were Forrest Hurd, Wally Warner and Bob Osmanson. Wally Warner was probably the big money winner when he took home $360 from a $1600 purse at Huron on July 4, 1950. Other payoffs weren't so good—like a total purse of $10 at a forgotten South Dakota town in 1948.

This Chevy Four racecar most likely ran with a roadster body at South Dakota races around 1932. Jimmy Wood was the driver. (Bill Wood Collection)

Unless noted all photos are by Frank Hughes from the Jim Johannson Collection.

This is big Pete Burnim at Mitchell in 1950. This car, powered by a 1941 Buick, began life as a Model T dirt track car in the 1920s.

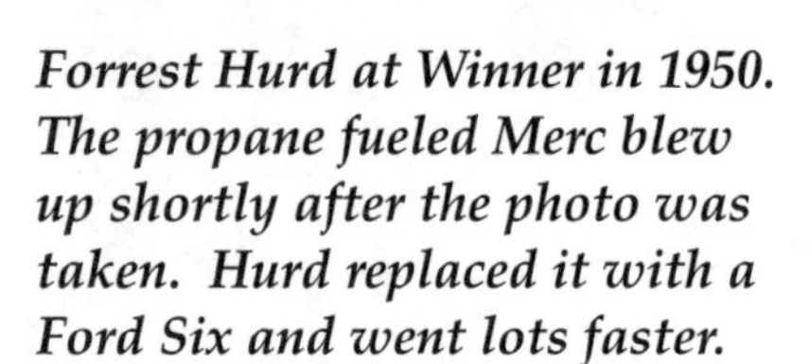

Forrest Hurd at Winner in 1950. The propane fueled Merc blew up shortly after the photo was taken. Hurd replaced it with a Ford Six and went lots faster.

Ernie Whiple is pictured at the Tripp County Fairgrounds in Winner. The Chevy Four engine came out of a 1926 racecar.

Two drivers battle in the dust at an unknown South Dakota track. It is unusual that there is no inside fence. Infield fences were hazardous but were useful navigation devices when it was dusty.

Sixty-five year old Pappy Wood was competitive in this Fronty T roadster. Here he fights a bit of a "push" at Huron.

S. California

There has always been a lot of racing in Southern California. This dates back to the Corona road races in 1914, the Culver City and Beverly Hills board tracks of the 1920s. Fabulous Legion Ascot ran in the 1920s and 1930s. Towards the end of the 1930s, there was a bit of a slow spell, but after World War II racing boomed again. There was Carrell Speedway, Ascot and now the fine Perris Speedway. Mixed among the better known tracks were dozens or maybe a hundred smaller tracks. The roadsters were a big part of this rich legacy of racing in Southern California.

A few of the cars that ran in the 1914 Corona road races could loosely be called "track roadsters" but the first true roadster race in Southern California took place in 1924. This was at a one-mile dirt track in Culver City. It was a race for "stock cars" but all were Model T roadsters and at least some of them were well modified. Bud Winfield, with his brother Ed as riding mechanic, won the main event. In the later 1920s, the roadsters ran exhibition events at Ascot Speedway (this was before it became Legion Ascot) and there must have been races at other tracks. It is known that there were time trial races at Muroc Dry Lake in 1927 and surely, some of these cars also ran on oval tracks.

In the early 1930s roadster racing got going at several Southern California tracks and there were at least three roadster groups formed. The most successful races were in 1932 on a three-quarter mile oval at Huntington Beach. These were sanctioned by the California Speedway Club and promoted by Bill Slawson. Races were also held at Riverside, Colton, Culver City and at Jefferies Ranch (Beverly Hills) on a track owned by former

This car has a wider frame than most and was probably built as a street roadster. Woody Wilburn gets ready to race at South Gate. (John Kozub Collection)

The roadsters get ready for the trophy dash at Huntington Beach. Promoter Bill Slawson is talking to the driver at the left. (Rich Slawson Collection)

The field heads into a turn at Huntington Beach and the dust isn't too bad. Bill Slawson, far left, won this race and a lot more at Huntington Beach. (Rich Slawson Collection)

A 1932 ad for roadster races at Huntington Beach. The track ran weekly races that were apparently quite successful. (Jeff Sharpe Collection)

Kenny Jacobson stands beside the wreckage of his Rajo T at Huntington Beach. Jacobson was one of the better drivers. (Rich Slawson Collection)

Jerry Mathews wrecked his T roadster at Huntington Beach. Mathews was probably thrown out of the car, which was probably a good thing. (Rich Slawson Collection)

Another wreck at Huntington Beach. There were lots of crashes and some serious injuries but no known fatalities during the 1932 season at this track. (Rich Slawson Collection)

heavyweight champion Jim Jefferies. Some very good drivers competed in the roadsters at these tracks. To name just a few there was Rex Mays, George and Hal Robson, Floyd Roberts, Bob Swanson, Mel Hansen, Roy Russing and Bayliss Levrett.

Starting in around 1934 there was a dry spell for roadster racing that, for the most part, lasted up until World War II. Historian Johnny Klann points out that many of the best roadster drivers moved on to the big cars. There was also the emergence of the midgets, which siphoned off car owners, drivers and fans. The economic effect of the great depression surely was a factor.

In May of 1936 Southern Speedway opened in South Gate—the half-mile flat oval was usually called "South Gate". Racing was with modified roadsters—cars with a narrowed roadster body and no tail section. Fields were good with good drivers racing in attractive cars but for some reason, during the 1936 season, the modifieds were slowly phased out in favor of big cars. The 1937 South Gate season opened with the big cars and, effectively, roadster racing was over in Southern California until 1946. (There was racing with stock roadsters and pre-1928 open jalopies at South Gate up until 1940.)

The first postwar roadster racing was at San Bernardino and was a bit primitive and unorganized. Racing was billed by the rather unglamorous name of "The Ash Can Derby" but the cars weren't as bad as the name implied. There were some street hot rods, some dry lakes cars, some leftover 1936 modified roadsters and a few cars probably worthy of the name of the series. The track was rough and dusty and the payoffs small. Future Indy driver Don Freeland raced there in a hopped up Model A and never did win any money—a fifth in the main netted a chicken dinner. In a way, the Ash Can Derby contributed to the start of one of the most successful roadster groups in the US—the California Roadster Association (CRA). Some of the Ash Can drivers realized the need to organize and they did so with the CRA.

The CRA was organized in the late summer of 1946 and held their first race at Carrell Speedway on September 1 of that year. To say it was a success is an understatement. Some 60 cars turned

BACK TO THE 1930s—OR MAYBE THE 20s

One of the splinter roadster groups that broke away from the California Roadster Association was American Sports Cars Inc. (ASCI). This was in late 1947 and their first race was on a road course at Don Mar Speedway in Norwalk.

In 1948 the ASCI ran a fairly successful season at various Southern California tracks. One of these was on a short-lived high-banked track at Fresno—Blackstone Speedway. (This track apparently scared drivers so badly it lasted only three races) In keeping with the group's "sports car" image, there were other races on road courses. In general, it seemed that the ASCI raced at tracks where the CRA did not have time to compete. The group did not have the big names but had capable drivers like Bill Steves, George Seegar, Bruce Emmons and Chuck Bruness.

In early 1949 the following press release was part of an article in *Hot Rod Magazine* : "With the racing season for 1948 behind, American Sports Cars Inc., is on the starting line for a performance as has not been witnessed since 1931. They are bringing back modified type racing. Old race fans will recall the three-quarter racecars that were running at Old Ascot Speedway that year. This will give old and new fans something to look forward to in 1949."

There are several errors in the press release but the idea was to bring back the modifieds that ran at South Gate in 1936. It also appears that many of the members of ASCI wanted more low key "just for fun " racing. At any rate, some nice looking "modifieds" were built. It really doesn't matter but the cars that were built were not modifieds—the term means "modified roadster" and roadster parts are used for the bodies. The ASCI cars had bodies built from scratch—technically, they were "bobtails" and similar to cars that ran in the 1920s before racecars were required to have tails.

It is not known how many races the ASCI ran in 1949 and 1950 but it looks like everybody had fun and that was the name of the game. It would be nice to say that the new modifieds were a big hit with the fans but that was not so. It wasn't long before some of the better drivers returned to the roadsters and the ASCI disappeared.

This is a bobtail—a racecar with no tail. The driver is Eddie Pullen at Banning, California in the late 1920s. (John Toprahanian Collection)

Jim Carpenter, on the pole, built an exceptionally nice modified for ASCI competition. Jim Ruth is on the outside in this Don Mar Racetrack photo. (Jim Ruth Collection)

The start of the trophy dash at Playa Del Rey in 1950. Pole sitter Jim Ruth won over Andy Anderson in a Studebaker Champion Six. Most of the ASCI cars used in-line engines. (Jim Ruth Collection)

Trouble! Jim Ruth tried out his car on the street and got nailed by the law. That huge tow truck in the background gets set to tow the car away. Ruth must have encountered a nasty cop—most of the time the law simply told us to knock it off. (Jim Ruth Collection)

A totaled car at Huntington Beach. With speeds reaching 80 mph the fragile cars simply destroyed themselves and tossed their drivers out. (Rich Slawson Collection)

Bud Tessien drove this nice looking modified roadster. It is really a big car with a cut down roadster body. (John Kozub Collection)

Another wreck at Huntington Beach—this time it is a Chevy. The three-quarter mile track took its toll of racecars. (Rich Slawson Collection)

Oliver Burton, with goggles, appears to be explaining why he crashed at Huntington Beach. Burton was later killed in a roadster at Culver City. (Rich Slawson Collection)

Pat Notary gets congratulated after a South Gate win. A sleek and well-built car with a Cragar engine. (John Kozub Collection)

up—most fresh off, or still on, the street. The drivers were almost all beginners, the cars were fast, so the result was a wild crowd-pleasing show. More races were held in 1946 at Carrell and at Saugus. Since there is barely a winter in Southern California the 1947 season started with hardly a break.

With all the racing savvy available in the area, it didn't take long for the street hot rods to become full-fledged racecars. Jack McGrath and Manny Ayulo were among the first to build lightweight cars with a Model T body, a setback alcohol fueled Mercury V8 engine and a quick-change gearbox. Troy Ruttman started racing with a hopped up Model A. It didn't take this talented driver long to move on to very good cars.

The year1947 was good for the California Racing Association as they ran nearly 100 races for a total purse of $180,000. There were races five to seven nights a week at a dozen or so tracks as far north as Fresno. They raced at the famous Rose Bowl. Purses were often $3000 or more. Thirty or more cars appeared at races and the group had over 100 cars registered.

This sort of prosperity couldn't be expected to last and it didn't. For various reasons that only racers understand (or do they?) friction developed and new groups were formed. By 1948 at least three new roadster organizations were formed. These were California Hot Rods Inc., American

Sports Cars and a Southern California Roadster Association—nothing is known about the latter group.

Roadster racing boomed fast in Southern California and it went nearly about busted just as fast. Stock car jalopy racing hurt, as did good ole TV and the move of professional football to the Los Angeles area. (The midgets and sprint cars were hurting too) By 1950 The CRA was in sad shape and most of the splinter groups had disappeared.

The low point for roadster racing in Southern California was reached one night in late 1950 when the CRA held an emergency meeting. Some 200 members gathered to decide what, if anything, could be done. The members were informed that the CRA was broke and owed $1000 to the IRS for back taxes. All hell broke loose as profanity and

A very nice looking modified at South Gate. Only a small portion of a roadster body is used on this car. The driver is probably Pat Notary. (Winkler Collection)

This is the Bill Hartgrove car at South Gate. Big car driver Bud Rose is at the left with hands on hips. Rose also drove the modifieds. (John Kozub Collection)

This is Bob Frame's Chevy. Frame, the son of '32 Indy winner Fred Frame, moved on to the big cars and was killed in one of these cars at Owatonna, Minnesota in 1947. (John Kozub Collection)

Troy Ruttman won a lot of races in the Del Baxter Merc. With Troy is his dad, Ralph, who was a big help to him throughout his racing career. (Toddy Ruttman-Kloos Collection)

Wally Schock built this car as a modified roadster. Fred Friday drove on this day and is at the far right. Friday later starred in the midgets. (John Kozub Collection)

The very neat Roy Russing Cragar. Russing later starred in the midgets and won a lot of races at famed Gilmore Stadium. (John Kozub Collection)

This is the only available photo of the "Ash Can Derby" races at San Bernardino. Spectators ring the track "protected" only by a barbed wire fence. (Walt James Collection)

Mickey Cory spins out at Saugus as Stan Kross tries to get by. Note that only one wheel on #14 is spinning—the rear end is not locked. (Hokinson Collection-Lovingood Photo)

Troy Ruttman's first roadster ride—his street rod. Although the Model A (or B) engine had an OHV conversation of unknown make it did not take Ruttman long to figure out his car was not competitive with the V8s. (Toddy Ruttman-Kloos Collection)

The Woody Wilburn Gee Bee Special. These modified roadsters are actually the ancestors of today's modifieds and super-modifieds. (John Kozub Collection)

shouting replaced Roberts Rules of Order. After a few minutes of this, all the CRA officials, from the president on down, walked out of the meeting. After a lot more yelling a bit of sanity returned and it was realized that a president must be elected—one who knew the sport, knew the people and who could work with promoters. Some 20 people were nominated and there were 20 reasons why they could not serve. Perhaps somewhat in jest, Walt James was nominated—James was in a Fresno hospital 200 miles away recovering from serious highway crash injuries. James was overwhelmingly elected the 1951 CRA President.

Little did the CRA membership know they had elected the best possible man for the job at hand. James started working from his hospital bed and the CRA was on the road to recovery. Roadster racing was better the next few years and in 1953, James talked the CRA into allowing sprint cars to compete. It became a completely sprint car group in 1957 (California Racing Association) and in the following years, partly under the leadership of Walt James, the CRA grew very strong and prosperous. Internal strife destroyed the CRA a few years ago but, basically, the same organization still exists as the Sprint Car Racing Association.

Many great drivers began their careers in Southern California roadster racing. To name a few of the really great ones—Troy Ruttman, Dick and Jim Rathmann, Pat Flaherty, Jack McGrath, Andy Linden, Don Freeland, and Jimmy Davies. Many more went on to race at Indy—in 1952, 17 of the 33 starters in the 500 had raced with the CRA.

Drivers who won championships in the CRA or California Hot Rods, Inc. were Jack Mc Grath, Troy Ruttman, Bob Cross (aka Bob Denny), Harry Stockman, Nick Valenta, Jack Gardner, Art Bisch and Dick Vineyard.

The aftermath of Bill Slawson's crash at Huntington Beach. The dent in the door of the Model A was caused when the car landed on Slawson's head and shoulders—no seat belt—no helmet. (Rich Slawson Collection)

Bill Slawson had been out of the hospital only a short time when this photo was taken. He is shown with Herb Orban who drove the car after his crash. (Rich Slawson Collection)

Bill Slawson is shown in the modified roadster he built and drove in 1936. He was one of the very few builders who used a Ford V8. (Rich Slawson Collection)

How often have you seen a photo of a '36 Lincoln Zephyr V12 racing? Bill Slawson drove this one in a 1936 Mines Field race—he was out with overheating problems. (Rich Slawson Collection)

Slawson gets ready to test the '32 Ford he has entered in the 1934 AAA stock car races in Southern California. Sam Palmer drove the car. (Rich Slawson Collection)

Bill Slawson was a man who contributed a lot to Southern California racing. From the early 1930s to the postwar era, he was on the racing scene as a driver, car owner, engine builder and promoter.

Born in Iowa Slawson came to the Los Angeles area in the early 1930s and opened a garage. This led to an interest in racing and, in 1932, he not only raced his own roadster but also was the promoter of the races at Huntington Beach. Slawson was the president (and owner?) of the California Speedway Club. He was able to organize the various car clubs in the area so that there was a more than adequate field of cars for the races. The first race at Huntington Beach was on March 20, 1932 and races were held every two weeks all that summer. (The roadsters raced at Culver City or Jefferies Ranch on the off weekends) The Huntington Beach races attracted some drivers who would be big names in the future—Rex Mays, Floyd Roberts, George Robson, Roy Russing and Ed Haddad.

Slawson drove in his own races. His car was a Model A with a Miller- Schofield OHV head—a typical "late model" racecar engine of the day. While the Model A was heavier it was no doubt more reliable than the mostly Model T competition. Slawson soon acquired the nickname "Cannonball" and won at least three main events. He was in the money (top three) in 15 of 18 starts. All this ended on September 25, 1932 when he suffered severe head and shoulder injuries in the trophy dash at Huntington Beach.

While no actual data is available in the purses at Huntington Beach, they must have been good for that time. A main event win probably paid $75. A racer who did reasonably well in the heats and main would go home with close to $50. It is believed that all contestants were guaranteed $5—not bad money in 1932.

After his crash, Slawson drove only occasionally. He ran a few times in the modified races at South Gate and drove in a Mines Field (now the Los Angeles International Airport) stock car race in 1936. He was a car owner in the 1934 series of AAA stock car races in California. After WW II Bill Slawson was active with the CRA roadsters—possibly as a car owner and surely as an engine builder. Later in his life, he promoted races at Jackson, Minnesota.

August 26, 1946 and practice day at Carrell Speedway. Don Freeland had run this Model B powered car at the Ash Can races but blew the engine on this day. (Don Freeland Collection)

Saugus in late 1946 or early 1947. Troy Ruttman slides through a turn in #37 as another driver loses it. (Hokinson Collection-Lovingood Photo)

Yam Oka in the #53 A-Pickup-Merc chases Orville Pruitt at Saugus. Note that Oka's car is still licensed and probably street driven. (Hokinson Collection-Lovingood Photo)

Orville Pruitt at Saugus. That looks like a Model A body but what is the chassis and engine? (Hokinson Collection-Osborne Photo)

Walt Bowen at Saugus in 1946. No doubt, this is his street rod—Bowen did not race for very long. (Walt James Collection)

A collision at Saugus in early 1947. Car #119 should be Ken Stansberry—great rollbar! (Hokinson Collection-Lovingood Photo)

Andy Linden in the A Pickup-Merc gets around an unidentified driver at Saugus. Look at that crowd! (Hokinson Collection-Lovingood Photo)

Right– Gil Avila is shown in a typical street-track rod. The V8 engine is in stock position and the radiator is in front of the axle. (Chini-Mahony Collection from Walt James)

Eddie Korgan leads Darrell Zimmerman in #28 at Saugus. With the wire wheels and knock-offs car #9 is probably a pre war big car. (Hokinson Collection-Lovingood Photo)

Orville Pruitt lands upside down at Saugus—no serious injuries. That's Lou Figero in #28—he later did very well in the stock cars before being fatally injured in a stocker. (Hokinson Collection—Lovingood Photo)

Yam Oka in 1946. The popular Japanese-American later drove and built some very nice hot rods. (Walt James Collection)

Lou Figero leads Northern California driver Gene Tessien at Saugus. Tessien is driving the Ben Hubbard car—the first lightweight Northern California roadster. (Hokinson Collection-Lovingood Photo)

Jim Springfield smiles at Saugus. He was one of many CRA drivers who raced only for a short time—were they smarter than the rest of us? (Chini-Mahony Collection from Walt James)

Action in an early race at Saugus. That's Jack Fitzel in #61 but the other drivers cannot be identified. (Hokinson Collection-Osborne Photo)

Manny Ayulo was another of the great CRA drivers. He and Jack McGrath built cars that were far ahead of the competition—until copies were constructed a few weeks later. (Swanson Collection)

Jim Rathmann (right) poses with his crew and the trophy girl after a win someplace in Southern California. Rathmann looks too young to be driving and may have been. The age limit was 21 then. (Hokinson Collection -Dayton Photo)

Andy Linden wins a dash in about 1947. Linden was another of the CRA drivers who made it to big time racing. He was seriously injured in a midget crash in about 1953 and never drove again. (Hokinson Collection)

Actor Leo Carrillo (center) sometimes served as master of ceremonies at CRA events. He is shown with the crew of the Del Baxter #20—driver Troy Ruttman at the right. (Hokinson Collection-Tanner Photo)

The hot rods line up before a good Huntington Beach crowd in 1947. Jack McGrath is on the pole, outside is Eddie Doran, Dick Vineyard is in #74 and Jack Bayliss in #66. (Hokinson Collection-Dayton Photo)

Balboa Stadium in 1947. That's Jack McGrath on the pole but why is he wearing Jim Rathmann's helmet. No identification on the driver of #9 or the starter. (Hokinson Collection-Dayton Photo)

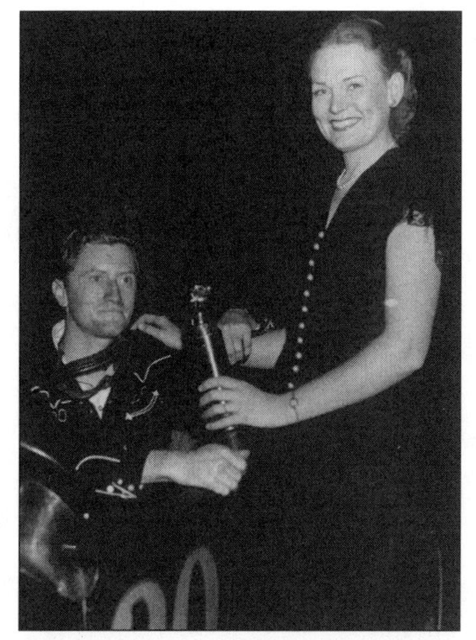

Pat Flaherty wins a dash—probably at Huntington Beach. Flaherty won the 1956 Indy 500. (Hokinson Collection-Dayton Photo)

Don Freeland (left) at Carrell Speedway in 1948. Freeland appeared at Indy 12 times with a third place finish in 1956 as his best effort. (Ray Hiatt Collection)

Two cars tangle at the "National Roadster Championship" race at the Rose Bowl in 1947. The race, with the usual CRA cars and drivers, drew a good crowd but the roadsters were not asked back. Cars sliding into the infield tore up too much of the Rose Bowl's precious turf. (Hokinson Collection)

Roy Prosser gets a trophy from a pretty young lady at El Monte in 1948. The car is the Reg Schlemmer Merc that appeared on the cover of the first ever Hot Rod Magazine. It has a different nose for track racing. (Jack Michael Collection)

Action at El Monte. Driving car #34 is Bud Gaus, #48 should be Leroy Nooks, no ID on the driver of the Ray Watkins #62 and Roy Prosser is in #20 (Jack Michael Collection)

A couple of cars tangle at Huntington Beach. Dick Benninger is in #42 and the driver of #39 is unknown. Benninger died in a roadster crash at Santa Maria in 1950. (Hokinson Collection)

The "Modifieds" line up for a race at South Gate in 1936. On the pole is Slim Mathis, outside is Shorty Ellyson, #1 is Rajo Jack and Tex Peterson is driving #31. (John Kozub Collection)

Shorty Ellyson's Mc Dowell. Nobody worried about those exposed fuel tanks. (John Kozub Collection)

Dick Vineyard in #74, Jimmy Davies in #29 and Yam Oka battle at Saugus. Davies raced at Indy and was a USAC National Midget Champion. (Walt James Collection)

Right– Colby Scroggin is pictured after a win at Culver City in 1952. Car 57X is from Northern California—owner Floyd Slayton is at the right. (Bob McLeod Collection)

Jay Frank was one of the better roadster drivers in the 1940s. Looks like he has won this race at unknown track. (Chini-Mahony Collection from Walt James)

Bob Cross (aka Bob Denny) was a three-time CRA champion. Cross retired to Idaho and played a lot of golf until his death in 1995. (Walt James Collection)

Leroy Nooks was one of the few black drivers to compete in the roadsters. He ran fast both in Southern California and in Indiana (Chini-Mahony Collection from Walt James)

The CRA ran a road race at Algoma, north of LA, in 1952. Al Getz is in #69 and Scotty Cain in #10. Cain's car was a throwback to 1946—a street rod complete with transmission and clutch. He finished second on the twisting and rocky course. (Hokinson Collection)

Chuck Hulse is another CRA racer who made it to Indy. He appeared in the big race five times with an eighth place finish in 1963 to his credit. (Hokinson Collection)

Al Getz won the dash at the Algoma road race but had trouble in the main event. Only seven of 50 starters finished the 100-mile race. The rough track shook cars apart and the rocks tore up radiators and pans. (Hokinson Collection)

Jay Abney raced mostly in Arizona and New Mexico but made occasional trips west. He was the winner of the tough Algoma road race but not in this car. (Walt James Collection)

Don O'Riley (real name Don Urgo) at Carrell in the Barney Curtis Merc. O'Riley-Urgo still fields a sprint car in Southern California and Arizona races. (Don O'Riley Collection)

Jack Gardner is in the very neat and fast #25 as Bob Cross battles on the outside. Gardner was the 1954 CRA champion. (Rod Eschenburg Collection-Faber-Stewart Photo)

Bob Dowell fights a push at Bakersfield. That looks like Rosie Roussel in the C&T Automotive Ardun. (Rich Slawson Collection-Faber-Stewart Photo)

Ouch! Jim Ruth gets on his head at Gardena Stadium. He was not badly hurt. No identification on the other driver. (Jim Ruth Collection)

Dick Hawkins was another black driver who competed with the CRA. He's shown at Carrell Speedway in the early 1950s.

Dick Mc Clung wins a trophy at Carrell Speedway. (Walt James Collection)

There are some fringe benefits to being the boss. CRA President Walt James is shown with a pretty lady at a Los Angeles car show. (Walt James Collection)

Don O'Riley is in #36 with Jim Gilchrest on the pole. This is Culver City in 1954 . Jack Gardner is at the right. (Don O'Riley Collection)

Jim Ruth's wounded roadster lies on the track at El Centro. Ruth spun out but had time to vacate the car before it was hit by several cars. (Don O'Riley Collection)

Jim Ruth in #11 leads Bill Cantrell at El Centro. Cantrell is driving a stretched Offy midget. (Jim Ruth Collection)

Jim Ruth spins out at Gardena Stadium in 1955. Ray Douglas looks like he's going to miss Ruth. No ID on #75. (Jim Ruth Collection)

Carrell Speedway in about 1955. Nick Valenta leads the way in #1 with Chuck Hulse in #14 and Don O'Riley in #36. That's Howard Gardner in the sprint car. (Don O'Riley Collection)

Tennessee

There was some prewar roadster racing in Tennessee and the neighboring states. All that is known is that the cars were "T buckets."

Postwar roadster racing got underway completely backwards in Tennessee. Elsewhere the roadsters were replaced by the coupes but not so in Tennessee. Bill Warden started the South Eastern Racing Association (SERA) in 1947 and the first races were with '32 to '34 mostly Ford coupes. Before long, tops were being cut off the coupes and by 1950, the cars were all roadsters. Some still ran the cut off coupe bodies but most wound up with Model T roadster bodies and were above average track roadsters.

Another win for Jimmy Warden at Tri- Cities. Warden ran a few NASCAR Grand National (now Winston Cup) stock car races—including Darlington in 1951.

The SERA ran a very successful and strong roadster program for several years in Tennessee and the neighboring states of West Virginia, Ohio, Kentucky, North Carolina and Virginia. Bill Warden was able to list 20 tracks where SERA drivers competed. Among these was North Wilkesboro where, until recently, major NASCAR races were held—it was dirt when the roadsters raced there. In general, the Tennessee roadster drivers raced for good purses. Bill Warden remembers winning as much as $500 in a race and as "little" as $50. (Had Warden raced in some roadster groups $50 would not be "little.")

While Bill Warden won some races, it was his brother Jimmy who was the real star of Tennessee hot rod racing. In 1951, Jimmy Warden won at least 21 feature events. Driving the very nice looking Harry Morris flathead DeSoto Six Warden won over half of his races for several years. Jimmy Warden also ventured out of Tennessee to tracks like Williams Grove and ran fast.

While most of the racing was in smaller cities, the Tennessee hot rods also raced at Chattanooga's Warner Park Speedway. Even though stock cars were running in the area promoter Joe Purkey drew good crowds by presenting the

Jimmy Warden leads the way as the hot rods line up at Tri- Cities Speedway.

"Hollywood Hot Rods." The announced purses were as high as $2025 with up to 30 cars on hand. The roadsters ran fast on the half mile dirt oval—Frank Moses set a record of 28.20—only .12 of a second off of Bill Holland's track record in a 270 Offy.

An ad for a 1952 Warner Park race states that "cars from five different associations" will be entered. Other pre-race publicity indicates groups from the Tennessee cities of Athens, Morristown and Kingsport would be racing. While it is possible that there were other roadster associations in Tennessee and adjoining states, it is not likely. Bill Warden remembers only the South East Racing Association.

Along with Bill and Jimmy Warden, some of the top Tennessee hot rod drivers were: Frank Moses, Bill Click, Paul Hilbert, W.A. Utsman, Bo Diggs, Willard Gott, Paul Prince and Tyler Calbough. Herman Beam, who ran with NASCAR in the 1950s and '60s, also drove roadsters with the SERA but was not a big winner.

Thanks to Bill Warden of Bluff City, Tennessee for most of the information in this chapter.

All photos are from the Bill Warden Collection unless otherwise noted.

A clever name for this Beckley car. The engine doesn't look like a Ford V8—what is it?

Bo Diggs is the driver of this SERA V8. Fellow driver Bill Click is at the right. Both men were winning drivers.

Tri Cities Speedway in 1952. Paul Hilbert (left) is shown with Jimmy Warden. Hilbert was killed in this car a month later at Morristown.

Jimmy Warden drove this Bo Diggs built V8 at the National Championship roadster races at Williams Grove in 1950. Warden was running well up in the field when a rock knocked the tops off of four spark plugs.

Bill Warden (shown with the car) and Harvey Diggs built this car for $1300. It was intended to be a combination roadster-sprint but Warden remembers, "It was usually protested when we ran with the roadsters."

HOT ROD RACES
MIDWAY SPEEDWAY
ATHENS-ETOWAH ROAD
Midway Between Athens and Etowah, Tenn.
Closing Hot Rod Race This Season
100-LAP FEATURE EVENT
Real Clean Sportsmanship by This Area's Most Capable Drivers and Some of the Fastest Dirt Track Hot Rods in the Eastern U. S.
¼-MILE DIRT TRACK
FRIDAY NIGHT,
OCTOBER 12, 1951
TIME TRIALS START 8 P.M.

This ad appeared in National Speed Sport News in about 1951. (Mike Bell Collection)

Some of the better hot rod drivers in Tennessee are shown at Tri-Cities Speedway. The back row, left to right is Willard Gott, Bo Diggs and Paul Prince. Front row, left to right, is Jimmy Warden and Tyler Calbough.

See Chattanooga's First
HOT ROD RACE
OF THE SEASON!
WARNER PARK SPEEDWAY
SUNDAY, AUG. 3
First Race Begins at 3 P.M.
Cars Entered From 5 Different Associations!

A Chattanooga newspaper ad. The "5 Different Associations" is probably the publicist's hype although Mutual Racing Association driver, Bill Brown, did tow from Indiana. (Mike Bell Collection)

The roadsters get tangled up at Tri- Cities Speedway in 1950. Although cage rollbars were not required, some Tennessee cars used them anyway.

The driver of this car that knocked down some fence at Morristown was Kittricks. That heavy body would have to be replaced if the car was to be competitive.

Bill Warden built this car in 1948. Obviously a cutdown coupe, it was one of the first hot rods in Tennessee. The photo was taken at Avoca Speedway in Bristol, Tennessee.

This is Beckley, West Virginia in about 1946. An unusual car to say the least.

An early SERA race at Island Park in Bluff City. The coupes are on the way out but one is running here against a couple of roadsters.

Owner and builder Harry Morris is shown at Tri- Cities Speedway in Blountville. A very potent DeSoto Six powered the car and Jimmy Warden drove it to many wins.

The roadsters line up for a heat race at Tri-Cities Speedway in Blountville in 1950.

Texas

As you may have heard, Texas is a big place. There was lots of roadster racing in Texas but it was spread out over a lot of territory. Chasing down this far-flung information has proven difficult but probably most of it has been collected.

As related in *Roaring Roadsters* racing got off to a

Lee Wick has a good sponsor for this 1932 race. Mr. Battersby, manager of the local Sears store is shown with Wick. (Lee Wick Collection)

good start in Texas in the early 1930s. Lee Wick supplied most of the details of what was billed as "Modified Stock Car" races in San Antonio, Houston, Corpus Christi, Austin, El Paso and several other Texas cities. The fields were not large nor were the purses by today's numbers. Probably one of the first ever-guaranteed purses for roadsters was at Exposition Park in San Antonio in 1932 where $250 was offered. Lee Wick won in a Cragar powered Model A roadster and took home $88.75—about two months salary for a working man in those days.

Information on prewar racing after 1933 is sparse, mainly because Lee Wick quit racing then. It is certain that racing continued in a number of Texas cities. Most likely, during the mid to late 1930s, Texas had

Chief Swinford began his long racing career in this Model A in 1940. This was probably at the quarter mile Devils Bowl Speedway in San Antonio. (Chief Swinford Collection)

Someplace in Texas, possibly Alamo Downs at San Antonio. It is about 1935 and dusty! (Don Bragg Collection)

more roadster racing than any other state. There are few years missing but in 1939, there is documentation of roadster racing in west Texas at Lubbock. Articles appearing in *National Auto Racing News* indicate there were weekly races with good crowds and adequate fields of cars. Leadfoot Brown was the driver to beat along with Dave Childers.

In about 1940 there was roadster racing in the Dallas area at (one of the many) tracks called Devils Bowl. This same group of cars ran also Grand Saline—some 50 miles to the east. These cars were a bit unusual in that they ran without brakes—see the sidebar for details of this strange group. At about the same time there was racing in Houston on a half-mile horse track.

Postwar racing got started at Spillway in San Antonio on an off-road course. Texans called this "Gravel Pit" racing and that's exactly what Spillway looked like. At the same time, in San Antonio, Devils Bowl was operating a half-mile speedway and this was closer to oval track racing. It appears that Texas roadsters were heavy with up to 300 pounds of metal for bumpers. One night Ken Stansberry showed up with a lightweight California car and taught the Texans that lighter is better. It didn't take long for Texas hot rods to become lighter and faster.

During the immediate post war period there was also racing in the Dallas area with the "no brakes" cars. A few races were held at Houston on the half miler and, later on, Playland Park opened and the roadsters ran there.

The dominant group in Texas racing was the Texas Roadster Racing Association (TRRA). This organization was headquartered in San Antonio and had some good races at Pan American Speedway. Certainly there were other groups but the only one that can be named is the Houston Hot Rod Club. In addition to San Antonio, races were held in Austin, Laredo, Corpus Christi, San Angelo, Houston and Waco. There was also a small independent group that ran a few races in Harlingen. Surely there were other small groups that raced in many Texas cities and have not been found.

Three champions were crowned by the TRRA. B.C. Ryan won twice and Henry Majors in the Don Bragg V8 won in 1950. Some of the other top drivers

NO BRAKES!

Leave it to Texans to come up with something different. Roadster racing got started in Dallas shortly before World War II. Many of the drivers were motorcycle racers. At that time, oval track racing motorcycles had no brakes—maybe they still don't. For reasons clear only to motorcycle racers this was for safety. The Dallas motorcycle-roadster racers carried this thinking over to the cars and brakes were banned. Some cars had no brake drums—some no brake pedal. This group also ran at Waco and Grand Saline. The no brake practice was continued until 1946.

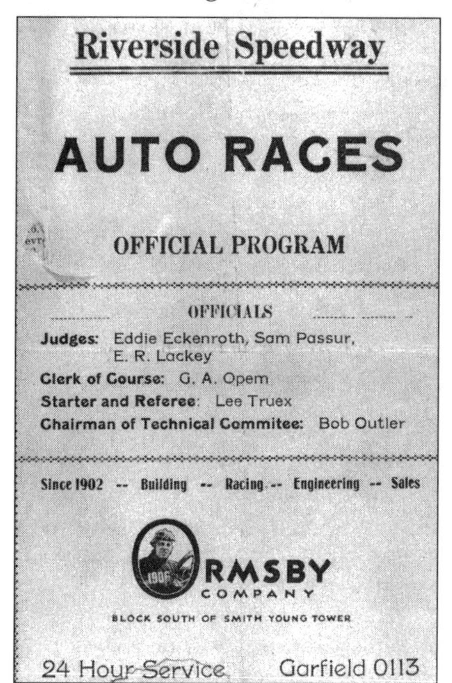
Riverside Speedway

AUTO RACES

OFFICIAL PROGRAM

OFFICIALS

Judges: Eddie Eckenroth, Sam Passur, E. R. Lackey
Clerk of Course: G. A. Opem
Starter and Referee: Lee Truex
Chairman of Technical Commitee: Bob Outler

Since 1902 -- Building -- Racing -- Engineering -- Sales

ORMSBY COMPANY
BLOCK SOUTH OF SMITH YOUNG TOWER

24 Hour Service Garfield 0113

Riverside Speedway was in San Antonio and operated in the early 1930s. The roadsters ran a number of races there. (Lee Wick Collection)

Lee Flowers in 1946. The Merc engine is in a Rockne chassis—a nice looking roadster but very heavy. (Don Bragg Collection)

WADE BEDELL REMEMBERS

Wade Bedell was one of the better Texas roadster racers. He also won lots of midget races. Wade ran hot rod races in some strange places. Here, in Wade's own words, are the stories of a couple of racetracks.

"Palestine, Texas. The strawberry capital of the world around 1946. Someone there put on a race ONE TIME. It was on a flat tract of land with some stakes indicating where you were supposed to run. The ground was hard red clay like powdered rock. Sharp as anything you've ever seen. I drove Roy Mc Call's #300 with a brand new stroker Merc. It started losing power toward the end of the race. After we got home we tore it down and found almost .030 taper in those new cylinder walls. The rings were almost worn out and the pistons were worn too badly to reuse. The oversized intake valves and the guides were shot. The heads were badly cut around the intake valves. On the tops of the pistons were deposits of GLASS—melted sand."

"Waco had a track in an old pit that was not bad at all. That is the TRACK was not bad. You got down in the pit and stayed there. The track was well banked around the walls on three sides and the #1 turn, which was originally open, had been filled and highly banked. However, the track was all there was to the operation. No grandstands, no concessions, no shade and no lights for night racing. The purses were fair and I made the 190 mile haul a few times and took their money." Roadster racing Deep in the Heart of Texas!

were Harry Elbel, Wade Bedell, Chief Swinford, George Carrvel, Harlie Morton, Cotton Farmer and A.M. Farris. Indy drivers Jud Larson and Jimmy Reece started in the Texas hot rods but quickly switched to the midgets. Another great driver who began in the Texas and New Mexico roadsters was Gordon Woolley. Later on, Woolley was an "outlaw" before it became fashionable—he roamed the country racing with a dozen different sprint car groups.

Thanks to Wade Bedell and Art Bagnall for a lot of help with the Texas Chapter.

Harlie Morton has just won a main event. This is probably Pan American Speedway in San Antonio. (Phyllis Morton Collection)

Good racing action someplace in Texas—does anybody know where? Chief Swinford is on the outside in #99. (Chief Swinford Collection)

Chief Swinford in #99 and B.C. Ryan ran what appear to be team cars. Very nice looking '32s!

Close racing at an unknown Texas track in about 1947. Chief Swinford leads in #99. Car #22 is probably Harry Elbel and #8 should be Lee Majors. (Chief Swinford Collection)

Charlie Morton drove in a few Texas roadster races. Here he is shown with friend Betty Fest. (Phyllis Morton Collection)

Jud Larson, Don Bragg and Paul Jett are shown at Pan American in 1950. Larson was already on his way to stardom and had time for the roadsters only in the winter. (Parks Collection)

The roadsters get ready to start a race at Lubbock in 1939. The photos are from a National Speed Sport News photo review. (Victoria B. C. Auto Racing Hall of Fame)

Some Texas roadster racers. Left to right is Roy McCall, two time champion B.C. Ryan, Marvin Brandt and Wade Bedell. (Parks Collection)

Harlie Morton drove this '27 T-Merc. This is Pan American Speedway in about 1949. (Phyllis Morton Collection)

Right– A special match race at Corpus Christi in 1950. Billy Rowland is in #3, Henry Majors in the middle and Harry Elbel on the pole. (Parks Collection)

Lots of help getting the Don Bragg hot rod ready for a 1949 race. Left to right are Marvin Brandt, Jewell Bragg, Paul Jett, Wade Bedell and (with cap) Don Bragg. (Parks Collection)

Gordon Woolley got his start in this none too sanitary car at Shady Oaks Speedway in Waco. Woolley later raced with the IMCA and was the 1963 champion.

Someplace in Texas—probably about 1952. Nice headers but, oh, that cage rollbar! (Don Bragg Collection)

Action at Corpus Christi in 1952. Harry Elbel on the pole and Henry Majors in #11. The Don Bragg owned #11 ran as late as 1960 in modified races with a cage rollbar and a Chevy V8 (Don Bragg Collection)

This is in San Antonio at Spillway. It is 1946 and the cars are primitive. The car in second place is a touring car—these were OK in early Texas races. (Don Fowler Collection)

Playland Park in Houston on Thanksgiving Weekend in 1950. This is the Texas Roadster Championship Race. Car #3 might be Billy Rowland but no identification on the other drivers in this tangle. (Parks Collection)

Another tangle at Playland Park. Henry Majors is in the Don Bragg #11 and he went on to win the race and the Texas championship. Dick Lundstrom owned #?. (Parks Collection)

Vermont

Roadster racing in Vermont (1949 to 1952) was apparently limited to three racetracks. These were Fairmont Speedway at Fair Haven, Griffin Speedway near Bennington and State Line Speedway in North Bennington. All are very near the New York border and attracted cars from that state. There must have been Vermont cars and drivers competing but none show up in the documentation provided by Les King.

At all three tracks the roadsters ran with the stock cars and were required to have cage rollbars. The roadsters apparently fared quite well against the stockers at Fairmont Speedway and seem to have won most of the races. Almost nothing is known about the roadsters at Griffen Speedway but, at the half mile State Line track, there must have been some potent stock cars as only New York roadster hotshot Wally LaBelle is known to have won a main event.

At Fairmont Speedway the roadster winners were regulars from Adirondack Speedway in West Glens Falls, New York. Wally LaBelle, George Dalbey, Hollis Hammond, Rod and Ray Therriene, Bob Lamphear, Bill McLaughlin and Bob Shardone all posted wins at the Vermont oval. Some "Powder Puff" races were held at Fairmont and Mrs. Bronk Hammond and Mrs. George Ringer beat the stock cars with their roadsters.

In Vermont roadster racing pretty much ended when insurance regulations required that steel plates be welded to the tops of the cage rollbars. The roadsters slowly disappeared and by 1953 they were gone.

Thanks to Les King of Watervliet, New York who was able to provide the only available information on Vermont roadster racing. All photos in this chapter were taken by Les King.

Wally LaBelle in his "Old #1." As at adjacent New York tracks LaBelle was a winner in Vermont.

Right–Rod Therriene takes a victory lap after a Fairmont Speedway win. Note the steel plate welded to the top of the rollbar—this was required starting in 1951.

Mrs. Harry Ringer flashes a big smile after winning a "Powder Puff" race at Fairmont Speedway.

Bill McLaughlin won some Vermont roadster races but on this day he came to grief on the way to the races. The car was wrecked on the highway.

This is really a stock car race but maybe we can call it the smallest roadster race in history. Russ Norton is outside in a Crosley Hotshot and track photographer Beeno is in the Crosley roadster. Norton ended up flipping his Hotshot.

Mrs. Bronk Hammond slides inside a stock car competitor during a Fairmont "Powder Puff" race. The gals went fast!

Ray Therriene loses a wheel at Fairmont. In one instance, an errant wheel at this track went completely through the ticket booth. The wheel neatly took ticket sellers' stool out from under her—no injuries other than to dignity!

George Dalbey's V8 is shown after a flip at Fairmont Speedway in Fair Haven, Vermont. While the cage rollbars were ungainly, they no doubt did their job.

Virginia

Roadster racing in Virginia began in 1939 at Winchester. This was with the "Barrel Hoop" cars that, for the most part, were unique to the East Coast. No doubt billed as jalopies, these cars used iron wheels off of farm equipment as rollbars. A few cars used full roadster bodies but most were hacked off at the cowl and the driver sat out in the open air. The engine rules were setup to rule out the Ford V8s but modifications were allowed. It appears that a successful series of races was held at Winchester and this probably went on until 1941. There is no doubt that similar races were held in other Virginia cities.

After the war, racing resumed at Winchester with more or less the same group of cars. In 1948 the Arlington, Virginia based Eastern Racing Association (ERA) was formed. This group, under the able leadership of Doc Benson, raced roadsters in Virginia and adjoining states for the next several years.

In 1949, Hybla Valley Speedway was built at Alexandria a few miles south of Washington D.C. This was a well-promoted track and it was hoped that the races would attract large crowds from the nation's capitol. The first race was for the ERA roadsters and a large crowd was on hand to see Ronnie Cash win the main event. The first few races drew good fields and, apparently, good crowds. On June 9, 1949 Ronnie Cash was killed when his roadster tangled with Doug Bailey's and flipped. At a benefit race a few weeks later Dick Frazier came over from Indiana to help draw a crowd and easily swept the program. The support from Washington, D.C. fans did not last and Hybla Valley lasted barely a year. (It did reopen later in the 1950s.)

The ERA raced at Manassas and Tappahannock in the eastern part of the state and had a less than successful race at Richmond. Probably there were ERA races at other cities but no documentation can be found. There was roadster racing at Roanoke, probably under the sanction of the Tennessee based South Eastern Racing Association.

This is a typical "Barrel Hoop" car at Winchester. (Frank Scheder Collection)

A field of "Barrel Hoop" cars gets ready to go at Winchester in 1939. Philip LaRue is in #3. (John Jackson Collection)

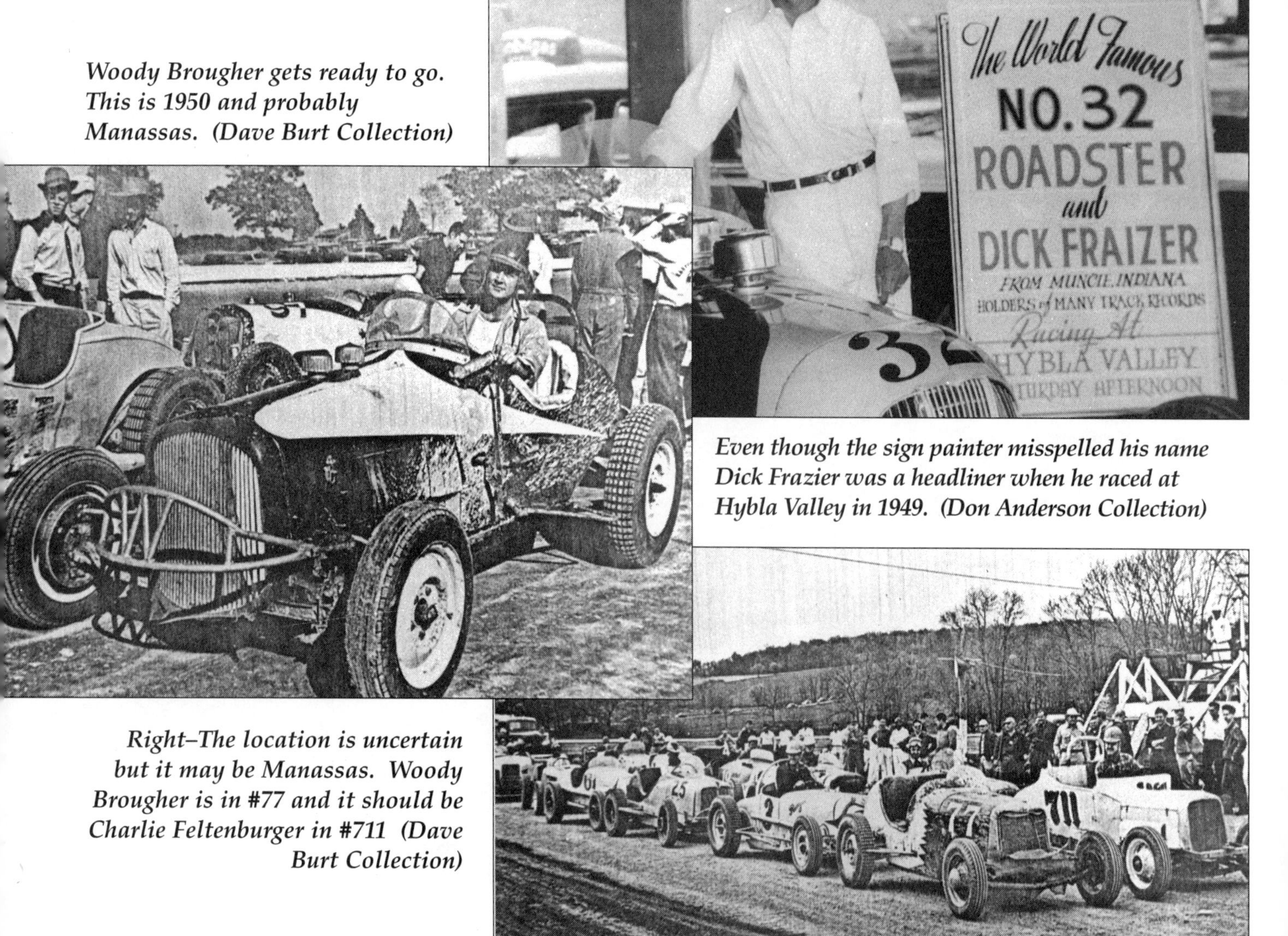

Woody Brougher gets ready to go. This is 1950 and probably Manassas. (Dave Burt Collection)

Even though the sign painter misspelled his name Dick Frazier was a headliner when he raced at Hybla Valley in 1949. (Don Anderson Collection)

Right–The location is uncertain but it may be Manassas. Woody Brougher is in #77 and it should be Charlie Feltenburger in #711 (Dave Burt Collection)

Washington

Thanks to Marian Dinwiddie of Roy, Washington, some information is available on prewar roadster racing in the Tacoma area. Roadster racing began around 1940 at the site now occupied by Spanaway Speedway near Tacoma. The track was then called Mile B Speedway and it was a primitive dusty place with no grandstands, concessions or even rest rooms. The cars started out as jalopies but apparently quickly evolved into true track roadsters. There was no group formed and the purses were small despite a hefty 25-cent admission charge.

In 1941 a Tacoma Roadster Racing Association (TRRA) was formed. This was at least partly the same group that ran at Mile B Speedway. The TRRA races were held on a half-mile track called the Steilacoom Bowl. A newspaper clipping reports that 25 cars and drivers were entered in a May 25, 1941 race. This must have been a well-organized group with some good cars but no further information could be found. In the Five-Mile and Steilacoom information there are about a dozen drivers mentioned. Strangely, none of these names turn up elsewhere in Washington racing.

Almost no information is available but about the same time the Mile B Speedway and Steilacoom races were going on, roadster races were held 50 miles to the north at Silver Lake Speedway near Everett. These events were added attractions at the big car races and there are vague references to drivers like Allan Heath, Don Olds and Art Scovell competing.

After WW II, roadster racing got started with a mid-1946 race at Tenino, just south of Olympia, Washington. A Seattle based street roadster group was involved with the promotion as were street rods from Oregon. A Four-Port Riley track roadster driven by Johnny Gorman won the race. (See the Oregon chapter for a photo of this car). A few weeks after Tenino the roadsters journeyed to the mile and

Flip Snyder at Aurora in 1948. This car surely started life as a street rod. (Don Haire Collection)

Yakima in 1948. Howard Osborne is in the #96 Chevy Six-T pickup.

Port Angeles in 1946. George ("Pop") Koch, center, is shown with his first race car—a Lincoln V12-Model A. Koch was a long time car builder in the Pacific Northwest. (Jay Koch Collection)

A view of the track at Port Angeles as a couple of roadsters get ready to race. This was very typical of some of the horse tracks the roadsters ran on. (Jay Koch Collection)

one-eighth fairgrounds track in Yakima. Andy Wilson drove a '32 roadster from Portland to the race, swept the program to collect $600 in prize money and then drove the car home.

A few more races were held in 1946 including a race at Port Angeles that turned out to be a real mess. The race ended with a crash that wrecked half a dozen roadsters, the ambulance was destroyed by fire

The roadsters line up at Port Angeles. To the left is Johnny Gorman in a prewar Four-Port Riley. Car #9 is Bob Gregg and on the pole is Frankie McGowen in the Koch Lincoln V12. (Jay Koch Collection)

The remains of one of the cars wrecked at Port Angeles in 1946. Of interest is the supercharger on the V8. Several Washington cars ran blowers but, in general, they didn't perform all that well. (Jay Koch Collection)

Parts of three roadsters are visible in this Port Angeles photo. The crash took place in blinding dust with an unknown number of cars involved. (Jay Koch Collection)

when a hot rod crashed into it, and the promoter skipped with all the cash. Perhaps all this helped convince the Washington roadsters that they needed to be better organized.

During the winter of 1946-47 the Racing Roadster Association of Washington (RRAW) was formed. The group's first race was at the Aurora Stadium midget track in Seattle and it drew a huge crowd. The purse was $3820 and main event winner, Del Fanning, took home $647 in cash.

The RRAW operated successfully for the next several years with Aurora Stadium as the primary racing site. Except for a squabble in 1950, there was cooperation with the Roadster Racing Association of Oregon and the two supported each other's races. (Individually, both groups were a little short of cars) The RRAW ran races at half a dozen Washington cities and, in 1949, made regular trips to Digney Speedway in Vancouver, British Columbia.

With the ever-present stock cars taking over, roadster racing in Washington went very much downhill after 1950. Fewer and fewer races were held and the last known RRAW race was held in 1953—only nobody knows where. There were a few roadster races held in Spokane in 1954 but these were with primarily Oregon cars and drivers.

The Washington roadsters produced some good drivers. Among them were Bob Donker, Johnny Gorman, Phil Foubert, Kenny Baxter, Pete Lovely, Mickey Sheldon, Lee Kirk, Chuck Cedar and Ike Hanks. Midget driver Shorty Templeman ran fast in the roadsters as did sprint car driver Del Fanning. Oregon drivers like Ernie Koch, Len Sutton and Bob Gregg won a lot of races in Washington.

Action at Aurora. Bob Gregg is in #1 and Len Sutton is on the pole in #27. (Jay Koch Collection)

Aurora in 1947. The original caption reads "Pink Lady as a roadster". Obviously a prewar big car—but who is driving? (Golden Wheels Collection)

ROADSTER RACING ASSOCIATION
of
WASHINGTON THRU' MAY '4

is to
ify That Flip Snyder

is a member in good standing with this Association.

President Sec.-Treas.

Flip Snyder's Roadster Racing Association card from 1948. (Don Haire Collection)

Another Port Angeles victim. Miraculously there were no serious injuries in the multi-car crash. (Jay Koch Collection)

You've Read About 'Em
You've Heard About 'Em
Now ... See Them on this Track

HOT RODS

Aurora Stadium
Tuesday, June 10th
Come Early Time Trials 7:30 p.m.

An ad for a 1947 roadster race at Aurora Stadium in Seattle. The hot rods drew good crowds at Aurora for several years. (Les Stark Collection)

Lee Kirk, center, is shown after a dirty Yakima race. The track was oiled dirt yet, somehow, was usually dusty. Car owner Johnny Mullenneix is at the left and crewman Bill Collicot on the right. (Mullenneix Collection)

Ike Hanks at Yakima—probably 1949. This car still exists today and is owned by Ray Hiatt of Hayward, California. (Gordy Sutherland Collection)

No—not Little Bo Peep. Del Fanning tries to cool off with a wet rag on a hot day at Bremerton. (Gordy Sutherland Collection)

Chuck Cedar in a very neat Washington roadster. Note the aluminum (four-inch channel) frame rails. These were popular on West Coast cars. (Golden Wheels Collection)

Right– Pete Lovely chases Bob Donker in #W2 at Aurora. Lovely is one of two roadster drivers who made it to Formula One. (Troy Ruttman, who drove in two 1958 F-1 races, was the other) (Gordy Sutherland Collection)

Aurora in 1949. Bob Donker is on the pole in Al Cooper's Merc with sprint car veteran Art Scovell on the outside. (Jack Greiner Collection)

Andy Wilson, at left, smiles after a clean sweep at Yakima in 1948. Wilson went very fast on this dangerous mile and one-eighth dirt oval. (Jack Greiner Collection)

Len Sutton in action at Aurora. This must be during warm-ups as both Oregon and Washington cars were required to run hoods. (Golden Wheels Collection)

Aurora Stadium in 1948. Track was somewhat "D" shaped. (Digney Collection)

This car was badly damaged in an Aurora crash. It may be Dick Brower. (Gordy Sutherland Collection)

Russ Gilbertson came up from Portland to race this nice looking '27 T-Merc. (Digney Collection)

This could be Ray Davidson who hit the very solid crash wall at Aurora. (Golden Wheels Collection)

Johnny Gorman at Aurora. Gorman also drove sprint cars and, as a machinist, built open axle rear ends. (Golden Wheels Collection)

Midget champion Shorty Templeman drove roadsters when things were slow in the small cars. Want to bet there is a Merc in that Hudson sponsored car? (Bill Hill Collection)

Len Sutton wins another dash at Aurora. This time it is in the Harold Sperb Merc. (Bill Hill Collection)

A somewhat rare photo of the roadsters at Sea Tac Speedway in Tacoma—they didn't race there very often. It is 1952 and Shorty Templeman gets ready to go. (Pike Green Collection)

Howard Shelly died in the wreckage of this roadster at Yakima in 1948. Shelly, who usually drove midgets, crashed on the straightaway at well over 100-mph. (Gordy Sutherland Collection)

Wisconsin

If there was any prewar roadster racing in Wisconsin the information is missing. In fact, it could be that a lot of the postwar Wisconsin roadster history is missing. Research in the last three years has turned up almost no new material.

The Wisconsin Roadster Racing Association (WRRA) was formed in 1948 and was active for a couple of years. The group had about 20 cars but, for the most part, these remained street-track cars and were driven to the races. Races were held at towns like Manitowok, Lodi, Edgerton and Hales Corners. "Wild Bill" Fitzgerald had one of the true track roadsters and won a number of main events. Other WRRA drivers include Jim and Bob Graff and Norm Hansen. It is probable that future stock car great, Norm Nelson raced with the WRRA but this cannot be verified.

At least two outside roadster groups also raced in Wisconsin. The Minnesota Roadster Racing Association ran at Menominee and possibly other tracks.

Milwaukee has always been a great racing town and roadsters ran a few shows there in 1948. This was at the Milwaukee Fairgrounds and the visiting racers were from Andy Granatelli's Chicago based Hurricane Racing Association (HRA). Hurricane ran four races on the quarter mile track at the fairgrounds. Dick Frazier and his famous #32 roadster won all four main events with nice payoffs—from $336 to $434.

A big roadster race on the mile oval (then dirt) was planned during the Wisconsin State Fair. Early publicity made the "big race" sound like a hundred miler with a "big purse" but this did not happen. A series of heat races was planned with a 50 lap main event. The 50 lapper turned out to be 30 laps, the purse was a flat $2000 and, once again, Dick Frazier was the winner.

In 1949 there is documentation that four roadster races were run at the Milwaukee fairgrounds. The races paid a total purse of $11,000 and Norm Nelson of Racine won the season point championship. The sanctioning body for these races is unknown—it was probably not Hurricane. There were two photos of the 1949 Milwaukee roadster action printed in The Midwest Auto Racing News 1950 Annual. Norm Nelson is the only familiar name. The cars in the photos are real puzzles. Cars have a way of becoming familiar as they appear in different photos at different tracks. Not so with these. They don't look like cars from any organization within a reasonable distance.

Another mystery is why photos of the roadsters at Milwaukee are so rare. Several noted photographers in the area have been contacted but none have photos of the hot rods at Milwaukee. They do admit to being busy with the midgets at the time but agree that many photos must have been taken. Where are they?

This is "Wild Bill" Fitzgerald at Lodi in 1949. A typical county fair horse track that is hazardous to both drivers and spectators. (Fitzgerald Collection)

Walter Champion flips at Milwaukee on June 22, 1949. Sim Sishkoff is in #2. The cars and drivers are unfamiliar—where did they come from to race at Milwaukee? (AP Wirephoto, Armin Kruger Photo from the Ken Parks Collection)

Roaring Roadsters Today

By Ron Ceridono

Track roadsters were among the most exciting and popular racecars of all time. Fans filled the stands of the nations racetracks to watch the topless terrors. Unfortunately nothing lasts forever and eventually the era of the track roadster came to a close. But despite the fact track roadsters are gone, they're certainly not forgotten and as testimony to their lasting impact, many hot rodders are keeping the genre alive with modern day derivatives. Some are virtual clones of the racers of yesteryear, while others are more contemporary interpretations.

Of course imitating the look of a racecar is nothing new. Even a casual observer can see that a number of the first Oakland Roadster Show winners were influenced by track roadsters. The influence of track roadsters (and that of their close cousin, the lakes roadster) has been evident on street driven cars for decades as well. The track-car nose, nerf bars, outside headers, roll bars, quick-change rear ends, big and little rubber and even four-bar suspensions are just a few of the items that found their way from the speedways to streets. So it's not surprising, given their rich heritage and the trend towards nostalgia cars, that track roadsters are again finding their way back to the boulevards. Many rodders are rediscovering the track roadster as a vehicle that is different, affordable, easy to build and most of all, fun to drive.

When it comes to being true to track roadsters of the past, few can match those produced by Marty Strode (Marty Strode Enterprises, 36329 N.W. Three Cedars Lane, North Plains, OR 97133; (503) 647-2603). Based on a tube chassis of his design, transverse springs are used fore and aft. In most cases running gear consists of a Flathead V8, early Ford transmission, and a quick-change rear end, although other combinations, such as an inline 4 or 6, are possible. Strode strives for authenticity

A great example of the inspiration a track roadster can provide is this home-built T of Gary Cross. The front suspension is based on Corvette A-arms with Bilstein coilovers. Brakes are Wilwood, steering is Escort rack and pinion. Wheels all around are 16 inch Corvette wrapped with Goodyear Eagle F1 tires. This car was built to drive.

Inside the traditional T-body are a number contemporary components including modified Fiero seats, steering column and wheel and '83 Chevy S-10 instruments in an owner-built walnut dash. In the best racecar tradition the doors are fixed, entry is gained by stepping over the side.

Marty Strode at speed in his Strode Special. What looks like a restored track roadster is actually a faithful ground-up re-creation. Strode builds chassis and components as well as turn-key cars.

in his cars, however the scarcity of some parts requires a few minor concessions when it comes to picking pieces. As examples, Volkswagen van steering gears are fitted and the bodies are fiberglass replicas supplied by Speedway Motors (genuine sheet metal is getting hard to find). But even those pieces get the vintage treatment. Racecar-style adjustable pitman arms are attached to the VW steering boxes, while the turtle decks receive custom louvered lids above and similarly ventilated pans below. Everything else between the front and rear nerf bars is as it was way back when: big and little bias-ply rubber, split radius rods, outside headers, tonneau covers, single hoop roll bars and seats that look like they just came from Army surplus.

There is no question that Strode's reproductions are as close to an original track roadster as you are likely to find, they're gas-burning examples of automotive lore. But the real beauty of his cars is they can be driven, both on and off the track. Throughout the country there are organizations

Strode's cars look like they mean business from any angle. Strode's personal car is equipped with a T radiator shell and wide-5 wheels. Ernie Martin's car (right) uses a chopped '32 shell, and '40 Ford wheels. Both cars are Flathead powered and street legal.

Another stunning example of a contemporary roadster is Neal East's T. East's is what was referred to as a 3-springer, two parallel springs up front with a transverse spring in the rear. What makes this car even more unique is that the front is underslung, that is the chassis is below the axle.

The rear view of East's roadster is reminiscent of early track roadsters and is dominated by the quick-change center section, tapered leaf T-spring and the handmade gas tank. Jack Presse of the Street Rod Place in Aurora, CO was responsible for building the car.

A truly contemporary car with track roadster heritage is this beauty owned by Brian Brennan. Construction of the Chevy powered T was handled by Darrell Zipp (Zipper Motor Cars, 2146 U.S. Hwy 6 & 50, Grand Junction, CO 81505; 970-243-6658 www.zippermotors.com).

that sponsor vintage races and/or exhibitions that are tailored to these cars. How much fun would it be to listen to a hopped up Flathead roar while getting sideways on dirt?

On the other hand, if cruising on asphalt is more your thing, just add a few pieces of equipment such as lights, horn and whatever else is necessary in your particular state, and you've got a one-of-a-kind street rod that's sure to turn heads while being a ball to drive.

While Strode's offerings are re-creations of a traditional track roadster, other builders have chosen to combine the old and the new in their efforts. Such is the case with Michigan's Gary Cross. A long time auto enthusiast, Cross has skillfully blended the vintage appeal of yesteryear with readily available, present-day components. Starting with a homemade frame, Cross blended Corvette front suspension components, an Oldsmobile Quad-4 engine, Camaro 5-speed transmission and a GM 10-bolt rear end on coil-overs as the foundation for his roaring roadster. To give it the vintage look he was after the late-model underpinnings were wrapped in a reproduction '27 T body and track-T nose from Speedway Motors. The result is a unique street rod with track roadster heritage and impressive performance.

Although the roadsters of Strode and Cross are vastly different, therein lies their tie to the past. Track roadsters were perhaps the best example of individuality ever seen in motorsports. Some were crude, others flawless as racecars go, while most were somewhere in-between. But the point then was simple enough: Competition bred creativity. Flip through the pages of this book and you will be hard pressed to find very many cars that are the same, the racetrack was definitely not the place for the cookie cutter approach. The objective then was to build a better racer by experimentation and the application of creative problem solving. Certainly the same theory could be applied to street rodding.

Building a track roadster for the street opens up a host of opportunities and this book is full of examples to follow and expand upon. Of course the real beauty of a track roadster is that they are basic in terms of function and form is open to interpretation. In short, they can be what you want them to be. That's what made them fun to watch and race then, and just as much fun to build and drive now.

Where Did They All Go?

Nobody knows how many track roadsters were built—a good guess would be at least a thousand. Perhaps two dozen exist today.

When the roadster era was over some cars were stripped of the engines and left to rust away. Since many were already basically sprint cars the roadster body was discarded and sprint car bodies built. Hundreds of roadsters were victims of cannibalism—racecars eat each other. Thus was the fate of many roadsters whose usable parts went into sprint cars—the roadster itself sort of disappeared.

A sprint car ate my roadster. The engine, gearbox, rear end and a few other parts went into the sprinter. The frame was cut up to make various parts for the sprint car. The body was put out in the backyard and forgotten. For some reason I've managed to haul this '23T body around through various moves for nearly 50 years. It still exists and, maybe, some day it will be part of a replica track roadster.

While no attempt was made to locate all the track roadsters that still exist, some cars did turn up during research. Some are very nearly as they were so long ago, some have been beautifully restored and some are replicas. All evoke fond memories of the "Roaring Roadsters."

Dave Norgaarden did a wonderful job of restoring this Tritten Buick. Check out the photos in the Minnesota chapter and you'll see it looks better than it ever did. (Harvey Porter Collection)

Up in Canada Larry Wendt has built this roadster replica. Like most of the old track roadsters it has a flathead Merc for power. (Larry Wendt Photo)

Rosie Roussel has restored this Riley Four-Port that he drove in 1952. He has added a bit of chrome, but the four-banger has not been touched—it runs just fine, so why mess with a winner? (Rosie Roussel Collection)

Bob Ginn in California is nearly finished with this GMC roadster. It is a very well done, from the ground up reproduction. (Bob Ginn Photo)

The Pat Gray roadster from Porterville, California. The car today is very much "as built" with the typical, somewhat crude, construction details still there. (Jim Montgomery Photo)

Ray Hiatt is shown in his GMC that is a replica of a car that ran with the California Roadster Association around 1950. Hiatt also has a Seattle roadster that will soon be on the track again. (Don Radbruch Photo)

Some restorations can be overdone. Not so with this Joe Graffio roadster—it was just as pretty when built around 1950. (Rod Eschenburg Photo)

This is an original roadster with a rare Riley OHV conversion. It was built in California, migrated to Minnesota and somehow survived to be restored by Dave Norgaarden and Harvey Porter. (Dan Iandola Collection)

DOWN TO EARTH INFORMATION YOU CAN USE, BY HOT RODDERS FOR HOT RODDERS

HOW TO BUILD HOT ROD CHASSIS, by Tex Smith
From one of the true legends in hot rodding comes the most complete and up-to-date guide on building hot rod chassis ever offered. This is the best and most up-to-date information on the subject. Included is frame repair, modification and construction, how to correctly install independent front and rear suspensions, solid front and rear axles; how to select springs, shocks, brakes and steering; how to make your hot rod handle and much, much more. Applicable to any make car or pickup truck, this informative book is written in the clear, concise manner Tex is famous for.

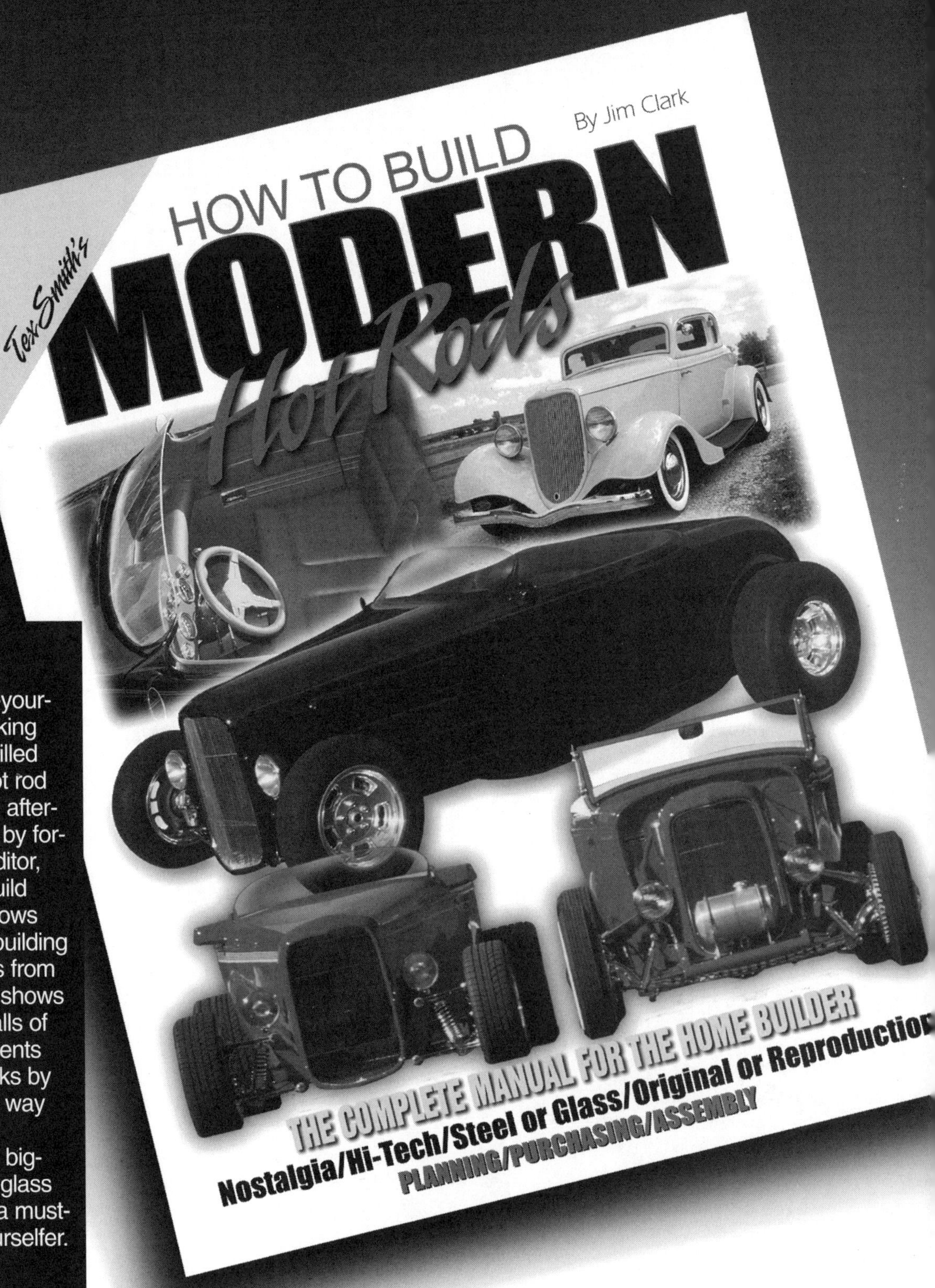
By Jim Clark
Tex Smith's
HOW TO BUILD
MODERN
Hot Rods
THE COMPLETE MANUAL FOR THE HOME BUILDER
Nostalgia/Hi-Tech/Steel or Glass/Original or Reproduction
PLANNING/PURCHASING/ASSEMBLY